Zap the Grandma Gap

*Connect with your family
by connecting them to their family history*

Janet Hovorka

Published by Family ChartMasters

Illustrations by Bob Bonham

While the author has made every effort to provide accurate internet addresses at the time of publication, neither the author nor the publisher assumes any responsibility for changes that occur after publication. Further, neither the author nor publisher assume any responsibility for third-party websites or their content.

Published by Family ChartMasters
P.O. Box 1080
Pleasant Grove, Utah 84062
www.familychartmasters.com

801-872-4278

For more information see www.zapthegrandmagap.com

International Standard Book Number: 978-0-9888548-0-2

Contents

Geek Grandma Knows That The Easiest Way To Plug In To Her Family Is Out On The Net. 57

Gifted Grandma Uses Her Creations To Teach Her Family About Their Past... 77

Groovy Grandma Uses The History Around Her Family's Past To Make Their Progenitors Come Alive.... 101

Gutsy Grandma Pulls Her Posterity Close By Carefully Creating Today's History Together. 125

To Mom and Dad

Now Grandma and Grandpa to my children,
you are super heroes in every way.
Thank you for passing on the noble heritage that we share.

You have made me so proud to be your daughter.

Acknowledgements

Thank you to Bob Bonham for the fun illustrations that gave form to the project. You can see his wonderful work at www.coroflot.com/bbonham.

Thank you to my editor Nancy Barnes for making this a much better book than it would have been without her help. You can access her brilliance at www.storiestotellbooks.com

Thank you to Lisa Louise Cooke for helping me realize that this was my topic and that I have much to say about it. You can listen to her enlightening podcasts at www.lisalousiecooke.com

Thank you to Erin Roudabush and Lara Orchard for being a fantastic help at Family ChartMasters and helping me find the time to finish this book. Erin and Lara are truly angels.

More than anything, thank you to my three children. They have been patient and adorable lab rats. As we've experimented with many of the ideas found in this book, they have taught me much. Being their mother is the most exciting, challenging and important work I do with my life. They are the center of my universe. Everything I do, I do for them.

And most of all thank you to my husband Kim Hovorka. He has always encouraged me in anything I've wanted to do and has believed in me and my abilities. I know I can always rely on him for support and for the best advice. I was lucky enough to choose a man who weathers the ups and downs with me and who has covenanted to work through everything we face as a family. I hope to always be worthy of being his partner.

Introduction

I honestly believe family history can save the world. When people are grounded in where they have come from, with an understanding of how past triumphs and successes, as well as sorrows and pain, have shaped their family, it strengthens them and empowers them. Family history gives us a broad perspective on the ebb and flow of life and the span of one person's effect in the world. As we come to learn about the people who helped make us who we are, who formed the family into which we were born, and who created the forces that shaped how we were raised, we have a much better framework with which to build our future. When we know our past we can make better decisions about our future. Family history can heal. Family history can help us relate to those around us in a more compassionate and sympathetic way. Family history can teach us how important our decisions are and how they will affect future generations. Family history can change our individual relationships; it can change a family; and thus it can ultimately change a community and even the world.

Whether or not you understand your family's history, it affects your life. If your mother grew up in poverty and fear because of the situations your grandmother faced and the decisions she made in her life, which were based on the way she was raised by your great-grandmother, you may not know anything about that great-grandmother but her life will influence yours. The strengths and weaknesses in your family can be better understood by knowing about that distant relative and the events that shaped her life. If your father was raised with a strong work ethic because his father was raised on a farm with hard working parents, who in turn descended from industrious emigrants, you may not even know the names of your great-grandparents or where they came from, but you experienced the effect of their lives in the way your father raised you. With a greater awareness of their origin, generational attitudes and character traits can be built upon or changed as necessary.

Learning about family history together creates strong bonds in a family. When you allow it to influence your life, your history can become a framework that protects and empowers your relationships. It connects family members in a way that is personal and unique to your family. Only your own relatives share your family's history. Sometimes it is the only thing disparate family members share. I have seen it used as a way to connect estranged relationships and mend disconnections in a family. It heals, it strengthens, it unites and it fortifies.

Because of these benefits, I am especially passionate about drawing younger people into their family's history. It is soul-nourishing for a young person to know about where they came from and to search out and be inspired by good examples as well as educated by the struggles in their family's history. Young parents who are not aware of their family history are missing one of the best teaching tools available for their children. Likewise, grandparents can connect to and bless their descendants' lives by passing on their family's history. Children are naturally curious and when they are involved in family history at an early age it can be a great benefit to them during their entire lives.

You may be thinking, sure, but my family's eyes roll back in their heads and they suddenly have pressing engagements they have to attend to when we talk about their past. You're in luck. Here are the real life examples and step by step instructions that will connect you to your children and grandchildren by connecting them with their family's history, so let's get going!

Inviting a child into the world of family history needs to be done carefully. Long lectures, lists of names and dates or piles of documents will not interest most children and may turn them off to the subject entirely. Family history must be introduced to a child in an engaging and interesting way that helps them feel the excitement and fun of finding out where they came from. This book will give you the tried and tested ideas about how to interest the children in your family in their family history and invite them to find out more. Some of the activities presented may work with your family history and some of them may not. Likewise some of the ideas may work well with your child's attention span and interests and some may not, but throughout these pages you'll find plenty of ideas that have been proven successful. Choose the activities that will work well in your family. Use these suggestions to spark your own ideas that apply to your family's history and your family member's interests.

Family history is one of the most important tools you can use to empower your children and help them become well adjusted adults. Like most mothers and grandmothers (as well as fathers and grandfathers) I want to give my children every advantage in life. I want them to be happy. Knowing their family history will help them find peace and contentment. One of the greatest benefits I have enjoyed as a mother is how moving it is to watch the breadth of the family I come from reaching out and then down into the next generation. When I take my children to see the playground where I played when I was their age, or the school that their grandmother attended, or the church where their great-grandmother worshiped, it gives me an understanding of the overwhelming length and breadth of my family and the effect that my life will have on the generations to come. It gives me a strong perspective about my life. The choices I make each day seem much more important. That beautiful inter-relationship of generations fortifies me as a mother and enriches my life.

In this book I'm going to introduce you to Super Grandma. She will show you all sorts of ways to connect with your family and connect them to their past. Anyone can pick and choose from these ideas to find what will work best for their family. If you are young, this book has fun activities to help your parents and grandparents teach you about the important foundation they have set for you. If you are a parent, this book will help you ground your children in their roots and give them the strength to become responsible adults. If you are a grandparent, this book will help you leave a legacy to your children and connect with them on a deeper level. There are sections and topics in every family's past that can engage anyone on some level, and when you do make that association, the benefits are immense. These ideas will help you and your children and grandchildren feel the happiness and power that comes from knowing about your family's past. Use these activities to bridge the generation gaps in your family.

Section One

Genius Grandma's
bullet proof vest.

Genius Grandma Knows How Important Her History Is To Connect Herself To Her Posterity And Connect Them To A Healthy Future.

It doesn't take a genius to know that today's youth need all the help they can get. Life can be challenging for these kids. The information and choices they face every day dwarf that of any generation in the past. So why would you turn to Family History to strengthen the next generation? Family history can help you connect with them and fortify them for the future. By its very nature, family history binds a family together and gives children a support system. It is something entirely unique to your relationship with each other. It is the glue that creates a tight bond in your family relationships. Family history gives children personal heroes to look up to, teaches them life lessons and gives them a broad, wise perspective on life.

Genius Grandma knows that by creating a support system of family identity, she can give her descendants the courage to conquer anything. One of the first things a super hero grandma creates for her children is a bullet proof vest. If that's missing, our little super hero isn't going to get very far. Genius Grandma knows that family history can be a bullet proof vest for their descendants that will protect them from many of the pains and disappointments in life. In fact, family history can ground them in the morals and values they will need for a happy and successful life.

The bullet proof vest of family history fits best around the ages of seven to twelve. At this time they are old enough to understand the concepts of generational change, and still young enough to need to be firmly attached to their family. When the bullet proof vest is fastened securely at this young age, it will stretch and mold to the child as they begin to grow into their more challenging teen years. At that point it becomes a scaffolding to strengthen their self image and their faith in the future. You can begin to teach your children and grandchildren about their history at younger ages, and it is never too late to teach them when they get older, but the vest fits best during the pre-teen years.

My personal bullet proof vest was hand crafted in the home of my grandmother. My father's mother was a skilled quilt maker. She made numerous beautiful quilts in many different styles and colors. Grandma usually had a quilt frame set up in the family room. My sister and I would play with our dolls underneath while she and Mom worked. I remember the needle coming up and down through the fabric above as we played house beneath. In her last years, she made sure that each of her grandchildren would inherit one of the quilts she had made. After my grandmother passed, each of her granddaughters received a quilt, except for me. Somehow, when they were distributed, we were one short and I didn't get one. At the time, I wasn't really upset about it. I had inherited several things from my grandmother. However, my mother was very frustrated that I hadn't received one of my grandmother's beautiful handcrafted quilts because she knew that was what Grandma would have wanted.

Grandma died in 1991. In 1995, when my mother was in the loft of the family condo one afternoon, she happened upon one more of my grandmother's quilts that had been overlooked and stored there. She had a feeling my grandmother would want me to have it, so she brought it home to give to me. Within the next few days, before she could get it to me, I suffered the miscarriage of my first pregnancy, a pregnancy we had long waited and hoped for. I was devastated. Mom brought me the thick, warm, corduroy log-cabin style quilt the day after we found out that the baby had no heartbeat. Over the next couple of days, following the resulting surgery and intense emotional despair, I had that quilt wrapped around me constantly. My hormones were adjusting and I was freezing cold for several days, so even when I went back to work, I kept the quilt around me. It was like a huge, warm hug from my grandmother. It became my bulletproof vest against the painful disappointment I was dealing with in my life.

Now that my own children have arrived, and grown big enough to understand, I have wrapped each of them in Grandma's quilt, and told them about how much I wanted each of them and waited for them, and how much I loved my grandmother. As we have cuddled under this quilt, they have learned of her sewing talents, but also of her consistent, cheerful attitude, her faithful service to her family, her adoration of me, and many other things I loved about her. I also tell them about my grandmother's mother, who was well educated and made sure that each of her children had a college education, even in the 1930's. Then, I tell them stories about other ancestors as well. A couple of years ago, by miraculous serendipity, I discovered a picture of me and my grandmother taken in 1974 while she was working on the very quilt I eventually inherited. I miss my grandmother but I am thankful my children and I can have a hug from her at any time.

Most parents today would do anything and everything to raise their children to be successful adults. There are play groups and preschool lessons, music and dance, sports, tutoring and youth groups. Many parents will read books about self esteem, discipline, setting limits and teaching a language. Money is spent on the right clothes, the right furniture, the right car seats, and the right nutrition, but many parents miss one of the most basic and foundational things that can set a child up for success in life—teaching their child about their family's history.

Family history can be a bullet proof vest for the heart and soul. It can surround and support family members in times of need. The courage that is found in their heritage will strengthen them as they head out into the world to make lives for themselves. Not all ancestors are illustrious, but every family has those who succeeded and those who didn't, and for every family story that hurts, there is also someone who overcame the odds and did better. We can learn from all of their stories. Genius Grandma knows how important it is to make sure that all that knowledge is passed down. When the power of family history is endowed on a family they become more connected, not only to each other and to Grandma but to a healthy future.

If you haven't found someone in your family history who is a scoundrel, you haven't done enough family history. Likewise, if you haven't found someone in your family who has accomplished amazing things, you haven't done enough family history. Every family has both. At the genealogy chart printing company that my husband and I run, we have printed thousands of descendancy charts for family reunions. It never ceases to amaze us how often we see trends running through family lines, even just in the vital information on a genealogy chart. Multiple marriages, divorces, and children born outside marriage may span generations on some lines, but when one person breaks the cycle, intact families follow. When pictures are added to the chart, the contrast seems even more striking.

In my own family, for example, there are lines of addictive personalities. I know I can't drink or gamble because becoming addicted to something is a trait that I come by easily. I also know I have several ancestors that could be described as overbearing. I would prefer to call them passionate. Any of my sisters would tell you that trait showed up again in me. Many of the attitudes and circumstances surrounding the way my parents, grandparents, and great grandparents were raised affected my parent's marriage and consequently how I was raised.

Lesson Learned

Every family has good and bad in their past. Sometimes in my occupation, I'm asked what to do when there have been abusive personalities and a succession of bad choices in a person's family. Do you really want to teach the family about the family skeletons? While there are certainly horrible situations that have occurred in some families, most all families have some painful issues somewhere along the lines. And in every trial there is always a survivor who overcame the insurmountable challenges that were given them. Of course, you have to gauge the age and maturity level of the child. If you teach about your family's history as lessons to be learned and focus on the resulting triumphs, the problems your family has been through may come to be the most important parts of your family's drama. Those may be the very stories that help and inspire your descendants through the hardest times in their own lives.

In my husband's family, it is easy to see issues that conditioned my mother-in-law to act the way she did. Her grandfather married and then divorced one woman, then married her sister, and is rumored to have fathered other children in their small rural town. As his daughter, and then her daughter—my mother-in-law-- were raised in that same small town, it isn't hard to imagine what an impact her grandfather's reputation had and why my mother-in-law was raised with a huge concern for what the neighbors thought. This concern for other people's opinions affected many of the decisions she made in life and has ultimately played down into my marriage and the way my husband and I interact with each other.

Understanding these trends and how they continue through generations can help us to heal and deal with family members in a more compassionate and understanding way. I have compassion for my husband because of my understanding of how his mother raised him, and how her mother raised her. I believe my husband is more compassionate toward me and my faults because of his understanding of the family that I came from. Likewise, we are both cognizant of the ways we are passing these attitudes and trends down to our children. When we make mistakes we can talk to our children about our learning curve in parenting. Some people say family history is cheaper and more powerful than therapy.

Steve Luxenberg expressed this understanding in his book *Annie's Ghost*. He wrote about how he researched his family history and uncovered a family secret that his mother had been fearful about sharing. He wrote:

> My search has allowed me to achieve a freedom of my own: free to see my mother as she was, free to embrace her flaws and accept her choices, free to put aside, once and for all, the pain of not being able

---

Lesson Learned

While your children or grandchildren may not grow up to identify themselves as self-proclaimed genealogists, they can still grow up knowing a lot about their family of origin. Every little bit helps. Any child can benefit from the blessings of family history because it can heal the past and inspire them. Each time they encounter their family's history, more and more of the benefits from knowing about their foundation will come into play in their lives.

to help her, to hold her hand and tell her convincingly, that, yes, I'm here, I'll always be here, I'm not leaving, I love you and no, nothing you say, nothing you tell me will make me go away.[1]

Understanding the pain and problems of the past gives us the perspective to see that most people do their best with what they have been given in life. In addition, we learn that everyone in this world, every family, has issues to deal with and overcome. Recognizing and understanding family problems and differences promotes emotional healing. Family history teaches children that they can overcome their own problems as others before them have.

The increased understanding that comes from knowing about your origins is the foundation of why family history can save the world. When we have an understanding of how past family problems play out in our lives, as well as an appreciation for past positive influences, relationships tend to become more kind, people are more generous with each other and the world is a gentler place. My great grandfather, Joseph Hatten Carpenter, a great genealogist, said, "One arises from the study of genealogy with a clearer and more charitable conception of the whole brotherhood of man."[2] I couldn't agree more. I believe the study of the micro history of you-- especially the history of what made up your own family--is something so important that it really can affect your outlook on life and the way you deal with people. It can be a crucial ingredient to a person's self image.

 Family Issues What are some of the issues in your family's past that you would like to see changed in future generations? What have you done to change those issues? How can you speak to your family about healthy ways to deal with these issues?

1   Luxenberg, Steve. *Annie's Ghosts: A Journey Into a Family Secret.* New York, N.Y. :Hyperion Books, 2009. pg. 350.
2   Carpenter, George Alvin. *Highlights in the Life of Joseph Hatten Carpenter.* Provo, Utah: Self Published, 1978. pg. 57.

Realizing Potential

A child's hero can have a great impact on the self esteem and the goals and aspirations he has in life. When that hero comes from the child's own family, an even greater sense of ownership and power comes into the life of that child. All families have inspiring figures that can serve as encouragement to help youth stretch and achieve great things. If you haven't found yours yet, you just need to keep looking, and when you do find them, be sure to teach your children and grandchildren about them. The self esteem payoffs can be huge.

Once, when my very scientifically-minded son was struggling over yet another dreaded book report, I commented to him that he certainly had it in him to write well because he came from a long line of prolific writers. After a while, he stopped the procrastination and finished the report. I am continually amazed at how such small comments encourage confidence in my children. Teaching them about their family's history is a wonderful way to inspire them with the potential they have to do great things.

A personal experience in my 20's taught me a similar lesson. When my mother wrote a short personal history of my great-grandmother, I found that my great-grandma had lost her husband to an appendicitis attack at about my same age. The history described her struggles as a single mother trying to find a way to care for her two children, at a time when single women didn't have the opportunities they have now. Her story focused on her emotional decisions about who to marry, her loneliness, and her concern about who would take care of her and her children. At the time, I was reeling from a divorce and the rejection of a husband who had left me after only a year and a half of marriage. It inspired me to know that the daunting trials my great-grandmother faced did not

---

Lesson Learned

Every family, no matter how many challenges, has good examples of sacrifice and courage in their past. What are the choices in your family history that led to good things for you now? Who are the inspiring figures that overcame great odds?

ultimately define her life. She went on to be very successful. As a child, I knew her well and I saw who she had become. I realized that my challenges, like hers, would pass into obscurity in time because I could see the whole span of her life. It gave me the confidence to go forward and become who I wanted to be without getting stuck in what seemed to be an overwhelming situation

I recently learned more about the sacrifices this same great-grandmother made as she built a business at the same age I am now. While I have been building a business of my own, I've reflected on her incredible work ethic and the way she just "took the bull by the horns" and did what needed to be done. This grandmother ended up with great financial success and quite a flamboyant style. I sometimes indulge myself with small flamboyant extravagances as a way to remember that I will be successful like she was. I look at my challenges and say "I can do this. It's in my DNA" even when things are hard.

> **Lesson Learned**
>
> Don't underestimate children's abilities and interest level. Working with children, I've been consistently amazed at how much interest they have even when you don't expect it. Keep in mind their attention level, tailor your activities to their interests and their age, and you will find that they will surprise you with their excitement about their history. If they aren't all that interested, remember it is all about how you tell the story and analyze the way you are presenting it to them.

Once while working with my children on a family history project about my paternal great-grandfather, we took some time to read about him and the great amount of family history work he did over the course of his life. It was moving to view the overall perspective of what he accomplished, a little at a time, until it became a great body of work. This great-grandfather was a wonderful example of scholarship and of being a great contributor to the community. As I read to my children, it felt like I was reading them a list of ingredients in their DNA. It seemed that I was reading about who they really are and what they can grow up to be. Of course, they are free to decide who they are and what they will become. However, it was very powerful for me to recognize that these good qualities are already in their possession, ready to be developed and improved upon in this generation. I hope my children will feel the power they have inside to be strong and capable adults who can make great contributions to this world.

All children should know their family history. We want them to be confident and to strike out into the world with a sense of purpose and faith in their abilities. We can send them out into the world with the broad perspective and power that family history brings: that hardships can be overcome, that good choices have long term effects on one's life, and that their choices will affect generations to come. As your children and grand-children come to know their family tree, they will develop the deep roots necessary to branch out and become successful adults. You can help them reach their potential by being willing to put every tool at your disposal to use toward that end--especially family history.

We have a stately wedding photo of my husband's great-grandparents in our dining room. Frantisek Josef Hovorka and Marie Josephine Kostal emigrated from Czechoslovakia to Chicago, Illinois, then to Wisconsin, where they raised their family. Under this picture is the statement, "What have you done with my name?" When my children and I walk past that picture, we are reminded of what we have to live up to and the sacrifices that have been made to give us the opportunities that we have. Hopefully, we will continue to appreciate and remember that we have been given abilities and opportunities to make good things happen in our lives and in the lives of those who will come after us.

 Inspiring Stories Brainstorm about the particularly inspiring stories of your past ancestry. Were there hard working immigrants or farmers who built wealth, mothers or fathers who sacrificed for their families, upstanding contributors to the community? What are the stories you can use to inspire your children and grand-children?

 Dealing With Challenges Do you have a family member struggling with extreme challenges right now? Look for stories in your past of similar trials and uncertainties that may inspire that family member with "I can do this, it is in my DNA."

Spiritual Serendipity

Megan Smolenyak in her book *In Search of our Ancestors* wrote, "If you were to gather fifty genealogists in a room, chances are that forty-five of them would readily admit to having experienced a few unexplainable incidents in their search for roots."[3] The other five just haven't experienced one—yet. Genealogy work of all kinds is filled with serendipity. Some may call it the numinous, psychic connectedness, luck, synchronicity, inspiration, intuition, providence, or a feeling of "I don't know why." Whatever you call it, most family historians have experienced the spiritual serendipity that accompanies genealogy work. It doesn't matter what religion you are or what your world view is. Some will explain that there is life after death and that their ancestors are interested and involved in their family history work. Others will explain it as an energy in the universe that awakens and heightens when someone searches out their own roots. No matter how you explain it, most genealogists can tell you about a circumstantial or lucky happening that broke through and helped their research and understanding. It is a phenomenon that leaves the family history researcher with a wondrous sense of amazement.

Stories abound about pertinent copies left in a copy machine then later found by a distant relative, or distant cousins that happen to show up at the same archive at the same time. Other stories tell of discovering some personal family history while doing general indexing, or randomly coming across an item about their own family in a book or on TV. Some of my favorite stories involve children and how their normal childish needs happen to put a family historian in the right place at the right time to find a new piece of information. With the advent of the internet and genealogy blogging, many such examples of genealogical serendipity can easily be found. Just search for the words serendipity or miracles with the words genealogy or family history. Several books have been written on the topic, including books by Megan Smolenyak, Henry Z. Jones, and Anne Bradshaw.

---

3   Smolenyak, Megan. *In Search of Our Ancestors: 101 inspiring stories of serendipity and connection in rediscovering our family history.* Holbrook, MA: Adams Media Corporation, 2000. pg. 1.

When I talk to people about genealogical serendipity, I have to be careful that I don't convey the attitude that the person's experience isn't unique. Working in genealogy, I hear such stories all the time, but every numinous family history event is amazing and special to the person who experiences it. When you put the stories of many genealogists together, lucky events in family history research happen with surprising regularity. Such events can give the researcher an enormous feeling of connectedness with their ancestors, and a common bond with other family historians.

I have experienced several miraculous events in the genealogy research I have done, as well. Many times I have been at the Family History Library when, after spinning and spinning through a roll of microfilm, I've happened to stop on the exact page where an ancestor is located. One night, early in our research efforts on my husband's Swedish line, a book on the parish we were looking at happened to open right to the family we were seeking. When I went back later to create a footnote for the book, I struggled to document our find because there were no page numbers and there was no index, not even a table of contents. With the research skills I had at the time, and my lack of Swedish language skills, I could have originally spent hours looking through that book and not found anything. However, when that page fell open to us, we were able to find information on two missing daughters that we had been unable to locate in other sources. While researching another family, the documents fell together so quickly and easily that it couldn't be explained away as a coincidence. I've often wondered if an ancestor was looking over my shoulder and pointing out where to go next. The best way I can describe the feeling when this happens is with the word "awe."

Lesson Learned

There is a long term perspective that evolves from learning about the history of a family. Often the "aha" moments come after years of slow and steady learning. Teaching about family history is a life process not a single event. Every encounter children have with their family history is a little more they know about their past. Encounters can be as small as a comment or as large as a full scale family event. Over the course of time, big and small encounters with family history add up to a foundational knowledge and an increasing sense of self for the child.

Often such serendipitous events happen after long years of searching. In fact, the long years of fruitless research are exactly what make these events so exciting. Just be sure not to get discouraged if serendipity hasn't touched your research yet. It isn't a matter of if but when. Keep your eyes open and enjoy the journey as you wait for your miraculous help.

 Serendipity Stories Have you ever had any experiences with serendipity while searching out your family history? How can you use those to create excitement in your family? Can you tell the story of your miraculous coincidence in a way that your family will become more curious about the people in your history?

Envelop Them In Love

Knowing about your extended family, living or not, can give you and your children a sense of belonging and being part of a greater whole. The life you have now was created in part by the decisions of the family members who came before you. If they immigrated, married, became educated, or had family issues, some of those events may have influenced the life you have now. Learning that there were people who loved you and worked so that their posterity could have a better life can strengthen your sense of self and create for you and your family a sense of a loving and safe environment. Our children can learn of the love those predecessors had for them through the sacrifices that were made so that they could have the life they have now. Connecting with relatives, whether they are living or have passed on, creates a community for the child—a web of people who care about him.

I once had occasion to attend an extended family reunion that my immediate family was unable to attend. I walked into the event having never met any of the people who were there. In an instant I felt at home and connected to a greater whole. These people looked like my uncles and aunts. They sounded like my grandmother. It was amazing to me how quickly I felt a part of the group. As I talked with some of the older family members, and they remembered and told me about some of my ancestors, I became aware that I was a part of a much bigger entity than I had ever before realized. It gave me a real sense of belonging in the world.

Lesson Learned

If you are excited about your family's history, and if you have a good relationship, children will be excited too. My kids joke that when they work on family history with me they get in my "good zone." My son says that I "don't notice their other evil plans." They know that after working on family history with me, they can talk me into many privileges to which I might otherwise have said "no" because I feel that their souls are fed and I can trust them more with other aspects of their lives. Hopefully they will come away from our time together with a love for family history because they love me. I have seen that they have already developed a love for family history because they love their grandparents.

When children have a chance to learn about their family history they often find someone who is similar to themselves. My son has recently been fascinated with his great-great-grandfather's old Amberola cylinder record player. This piece of machinery, invented by Thomas Edison, was a technological marvel in its day. It has resonated with my son because of his interest in modern tech gadgets, inventions and toys. He has found common ground with his great-great-grandfather--an interest in the latest technology and interesting inventions. Other children might find people who look like them, or have common talents and interests such as music, sports or hobbies. Finding a relative with similar interests makes one feel a part of something bigger than ourselves.

Family history also has a personal, present-day binding effect on families. As you work on your family history with your children, they not only learn more about their ancestors, they also learn about and become closer to you. Family history can be common ground for family members who might appear to share little else in common. Family projects and even family mysteries can create a family gathering place as members can work together and share a common goal and common experience.

Likewise, family history is often a solace for people whose current family ties aren't what they would like them to be. I once knew a woman who was obsessed with family history because it gave her a sense of stability when she lived far away from home. When her husband's work necessitated family moves every year or so, she found that ties to her ancestors gave her the connection she was rarely able to establish in short-lived relationships with neighbors and friends. Likewise, people often come to genealogy when there is a loss of a close family member and they are longing to know more about the person they have lost. (Some people even find that it is easier to deal with dead relatives than with the ones who are living.) Family history gives a person a solid foundation and the security of knowing who they are.

Lesson Learned

Family history is best passed down when you understand the family members you are trying to involve. Know the attention span of the children you are working with. Know how they approach problems and what frustrates them. Know what interests and hobbies they have that might tie in to a project you want to do. Find a characteristic they have in common with an ancestor. When you bring the family history to the child rather than try to bring the child to the family history, your child's connection will be much stronger and easier to forge.

Strong Relationships What can you do in general to strengthen the relationships you have with your children or grandchildren? Time spent together? Letters, e-mails, or texts? Can you be more interested in the hobbies that they have? Can you trade time spent on their hobby for time spent on your family history? What hobbies of theirs can you show more interest in?

 Common Interests What hobbies and interests do your family members have now that correlate with the hobbies and interests of your ancestors? Do you have a child who is interested in fashion? Do you have a child interested in weapons and wars? Do you have a child interested in animals or writing or cooking? How do these interests fit into your family history?

A Broad Perspective

Learning about family history reminds us that we aren't just the sum of the current life issues we are dealing with. Family history helps us gain a broader perspective of life—and even generations of lives. Knowing that our ancestor's decisions affect our lives, where we were born, and the opportunities we have, we can teach youth that the decisions they make will ultimately effect the following generations. Personally, I find I make better decisions when I remember that what I am doing now not only affects me but other family members as well.

Several years ago, I had been running errands and came home to find our washing machine hose had exploded and our house was flooding. The water was about 4 inches deep on the main floor and it was raining downstairs through the furnace ducts. The basement already had about 2-3 inches of water. Of course it wasn't a day where the house was cleaned up, and as I frantically started picking things up to rescue them, I remember thinking "Oh no, what am I going to do?" As I surveyed the dining room in the middle of that mess, I glanced up to where we had hung several genealogy charts, and I experienced an important moment. I saw the photos of my ancestors who had lived through the depression, served in wars, crossed the plains, emigrated and survived all sorts of calamities. I stopped in my tracks as an overwhelming understanding came over me. I realized that my current crisis was not that big a deal. I had insurance and things would be taken care of. The rest of the week was arguably one of the most stressful weeks of my life: I had to leave town on business,

---

Lesson Learned

If family history is boring you are doing it wrong. When your children or grandchildren are bored, look for something that will connect them with what they are already interested in. Family History involves so many topics. There is always another avenue to explore. Any one of us would be interested in seeing a picture of a great-grandfather who looked just like us, and any child would like to see his grandfather's school report card when he was their age. All children will listen to stories about the trouble their mother got into as a child. Keep trying until you find the topic that makes them say "hmmm" or even "wow."

---

my daughter was sick and taken to the hospital, and all of our carpet and our entire kitchen had to be ripped out and replaced. With my new broadened perspective, I went through that week with much more of a sense of calm and perspective than I would have had otherwise.

Aside from all of the benefits cited above, there are also many other skills and abilities that family history can teach us and our children. Family history research involves logic, detective skills, library and research skills, writing and communication. It also involves spelling, typing and computer skills. It involves organization and the ability to sift and judge information based on its source. This kind of micro historical research can give children a context for other historical, geographical and cultural knowledge. It can help make history come alive when historical events they learn about in school are coupled with stories of family members who were involved or lived at the same time. It can teach them vital, valuable skills to use in school and later in the workplace.

Lesson Learned

Don't over program your children and grandchildren. Just let them be curious. With the huge wealth of information that encompasses your family history, there is something to interest everyone. What small part of your family history can you tell them about to spark some curiosity? How can you encourage them to find out more for themselves? Even if you think you know everything about a particular part of your family, you'll be amazed if you stand back and watch where your descendants go with it.

Family history holds such a wealth of learning for children and young people that I've often thought it would be a wonderful basis for a year-long homeschooling curriculum based on the child's own personal family history. Just think what that curriculum could envelop: history, geography, language, religion, culture, art, music, research skills, communication skills, and computer skills. Who knows how many subjects you could include? If our family had possessed the constitution and stamina to be a homeschooling family, that would have been the greatest fun. Perhaps it is something your family could do.

Family history can also create new interests. Many writers have been inspired by their family history. Margaret Mitchell based her book *Gone with the Wind* on the stories she heard her aunts and uncles telling as she grew up. In fact, many great authors have based their writings on what they know the best--the people and places where they grew up. Family history can give children a strong foundation on which to base their understanding of the world around them. It can give them ideas and awareness to build and create new knowledge.

Ideally, as children learn about the sacrifices that were made on their behalf and the hardships that were commonplace in earlier times, family history can instill a great sense of gratitude for the comforts we enjoy in modern times. Simply understanding what it was like to homestead, to have an outhouse, or to live with diseases or child labor can increase a child's appreciation for the basic comforts and opportunities that we take for granted.

 Start With The Child Bring the family history to the child, not the child to family history. Don't start with what you know about your ancestors; start with what you know about your child. What are their interests? What do they get excited about? Now look for aspects of that interest in your family history. Do you have a child that is interested in sports? Do you have family members who were athletic? Do you have a child interested in animals? What do you know about animals that your family members may have owned? What are the cultural or historical events and circumstances surrounding your family's past that may help a child gain perspective on his or her family members?

Section Two

Gorgeous Grandma's superior vision goggles.

Gorgeous Grandma Infuses Her Surroundings With Her Family History To Instill Her Family With Their Past And Prepare Them For Later Curiosity.

There are many things competing for your family's attention in this fast paced world. It seems that everything glitters and seduces. How can you make your family history attractive and help it grab the attention of your family members? What will bring your ancestors the consideration they deserve? To start with, make sure you show your family how gorgeous your family history is by visually surrounding them with their heritage.

Gorgeous Grandma knows just what her family needs. An essential super hero device is a good pair of goggles. Goggles are the means by which you see the world, and through which Gorgeous Grandma helps her children see their family history. This is an inconspicuous way to bring family history into a family's life without having to say a word. When she surrounds them with their gorgeous family history, they will begin to learn about their past in their peripheral vision and may not even realize they are doing it.

Gorgeous Grandma will make sure that her family history pictures are out where the family can see them all the time. They might be on a bookshelf, or on the piano, or on the wall. She also proudly displays any heirlooms she may have inherited and usually has them labeled or displayed alongside a picture of the original owner. Gorgeous Grandma knows the value of charts and maps to add the time frame and geographical location to her family history displays. Her family history may even spread out to the landscaping surrounding her home. In fact, Gorgeous Grandma knows that making her family's past a pronounced part of the design in and around her home not only inspires familiarity in her family members, but might even create curiosity in other visitors as well. She'll likely inspire those other guests to learn more about their own family's past.

My goggles were fashioned by my mother, perhaps accidentally. I don't know that either one of us realized what Mom was instinctively doing in our peripheral vision. She didn't really start officially including her children in her projects until my younger sisters came along and I was older. I don't remember my mother ever taking me to the Family History Library. I don't remember her ever organizing a family history "event" for my benefit. I don't think we ever celebrated an ancestor's birthday or created a family history bingo game. The way Mom imbued me with family history was just by being who she was. She was a person who was very connected to her family's past. She just lived it. She was someone who was vested and interested in collecting it.

What I remember the most about how she gave me the desire to be a family historian is that she always had family history pictures on display in our home. The people in those pictures are real to me. Their presence in our home gave me the foundation for all of the other history that came up naturally in our lives. There were also charts on the wall and heirlooms on the bookshelves. Interestingly, the choices my mother made because of how she had been raised had context because of those pictures on the wall. Family history was so infused in her life, and thus in mine, that neither one of us can really remember all the little moments when she taught me something about where I came from. She probably wouldn't remember how she taught me to lick my thumb and stamp it into the palm of the other hand for good luck every time I see a white horse, just like her grandmother Viola taught her. Nor would she remember how she taught me to hold a dandelion under someone's chin to see if they like butter, or how to sing "A you're Adorable, B you're so Beautiful, C you're a Cutie full of charms" like Nama did. But I knew what my ancestors looked like and I knew something about what they did. Even if I had never realized I knew much about my family history, I would have been strengthened by it because of my mother's influence. For many, many years I wasn't interested, but eventually, just by the way she lived and what she surrounded me with in my life, I gained a love for my ancestors.

In the following pages you will find specifics about how to make your family's history a gorgeous part of your surroundings. Help your family members have a more beautiful outlook on life by helping them see the world through the goggles of family history. It can be a powerful part of their own super hero suit.

Visuals/Pictures

Your most powerful ally in the quest to zap the grandma gap and help your family connect to their ancestors is your visual history. This is the place to start with your children and grandchildren. It is true that a picture is worth a thousand words. Pictures make the past come alive with visual images of how your ancestors looked, how they dressed, their surroundings and their activities. Pictures give us a reference on which to hang all other stories and activities. Your ancestors become real people who moved and talked, had relationships and even primped for a camera.

Photography was first available in the 1830s, and by the mid 1800's its popularity had spread to the common man. Consequently, you probably only have four or five generations of pictures if you are very lucky. Most people aren't that lucky, and really only have pictures of the last couple of generations. Pictures of your family history probably multiply in the mid 1900s as commercial photography became popular, so you are going to have a lot of resources from the last generation or two and less as you go further back in time. However, if you have any pictures at all, you have enough to get started with. Often the mere exercise of beginning to collect photos attracts more. Pick a few that are the most important photos in your family's history and start there. Wedding pictures and professional portraits taken at important life stages are a good place to start.

Family pictures are useful when safe and protected in the family scrapbook or other family history book, but they are most useful out where your family members and your visitors see them daily in your home. This can easily be accomplished with today's assortment of scanners, printers, and copiers. When you use your family history to decorate your home, your family members naturally come to know the images as a part of their surroundings. Without ever saying a word, the pictures can be the starting point for your family's connections to their family history.

Whenever my family moved, an appropriate wall was found to display family history pictures. We always had two displays. One was the year to year school portraits for each of us as children. Later, it became a wall of family portraits progressing through time from the bouffant hairdos of the sixties to the bicentennial pinafores of the seventies, to the swoopy bangs of the eighties, to the short techno-bobs in the nineties and on, into the present. These photos of myself and my sisters were very important to me, but the wall I remember most was the wall that started with my parent's wedding picture, then branched out to the wedding pictures of their parents, and so on back to my great-great grandparents. Some of the older pictures are not wedding pictures of course, but all of them are labeled with names. Over the years, as I passed that wall, I learned who each of those people were. I knew what they looked like. I identified with them because I could see something of them in my parents and in me and that gave me the context to build on when I heard stories or participated in traditions. I identified with my ancestors because I looked like them and they were a part of me.

When you are utilizing your images, look especially for pictures with a family resemblance. Anyone is captivated to find the picture of an ancestor who looked similar to them or similar to one of their living family members. Even adopted children can relate to the photos of ancestors of the parents they love and who have raised them. A visual connection to a person creates a bond and fosters curiosity. Likewise, look for intriguing details around a person, the fashion, the hairstyles, and the context that might give clues to the ancestor's personality, time period or location. Become educated about these details and share those stories with your family. Books by author Maureen Taylor and other books on dating old photographs will give you hints and specifics about how to draw out a longing in your children to learn more.

Once, when I was going through my husband's family pictures, I was surprised to find a picture of my husband and his brother in sailor suits at the ages of around 4 and 6. I recognized it as similar to one of my family pictures with my father and his brother in a much earlier time period, but with very similar sailor suits. When I was blessed with two little boys of my own, we took them to get their pictures taken, in sailor suits, at about the same ages. We turned the serendipity of two similar pictures from different family lines into a family tradition that I hope will connect my boys back through the generations.

Displays Create a display of ancestor pictures. Contact everyone you know who might have old photos of your family – both family members and family friends. Search the internet, the library and your own belongings. Pick out 10 to 15 pictures from your family's history and make copies to frame. Decorate your house with these pictures on the piano, on the bookshelves, on the wall. Use matting or decorative papers to label the pictures with names and, if possible, a date. Arrange the pictures in chronological order or by lineage. Be sure that you use copies of the pictures and store originals in a place where they won't be damaged by light or dust.

 Timelines Arrange pictures of your current family in a timeline. Create a timeline of pictures connecting the lives of your children and their living ancestors. Start with baby pictures of the child and display a picture from each year of his life. Or, you can start with baby pictures of the child's parents and use periodic pictures throughout their life to come up to the present, including the birth of the children in the family. Again, be sure to use copies of the pictures and store originals in a place where they won't be damaged by light or dust.

 Similarities Exhibit pictures of ancestors who look similar to your children, their cousins or aunts and uncles, or pictures which place their ancestors in a similar context. Do you have any pictures of ancestors at the ages your children are now? Do you have any pictures with similar activities or characteristics? Display these and create matching pictures of your children doing those activities now.

Heirlooms

In most families there are a few treasured heirlooms that have been kept and passed down through the generations. These may be items which were precious to the people who originally owned them, or they may have become more precious because of the time which has passed. Some of the heirlooms in my family include shoe repair tools, porcelain cats, wedding cake toppers, and perfume bottles, but more common heirlooms might include jewelry, dishes and silver sets, clothing or furniture.

Heirlooms can be useful to encourage curiosity and create context for your ancestors' lives. A physical item that was used by your ancestors brings their lives into the present. Some may keep an heirloom packed away for safety reasons, but it is possible to display an heirloom in a safe but visible place in the home for people to enjoy. The tops of cupboards, inside china cabinets or bookshelves are great places to display family heirlooms.

In my mom and dad's bedroom when I was growing up, there was a cedar chest full of treasures from my family history. It contained a doll that my great-great-grandmother made for my mother when she was born. As my sisters and I grew, Mom added our blessing dresses and other special dresses that she made for us. The clothes my parents wore to their wedding were in the chest as well as several crocheted doilies that my grandmothers and great-grandmothers had made.

The oldest and most treasured thing in that chest, to me, was a handkerchief made by my mother's mother's mother's mother's mother. Yes, it's that old. My 4th great-grandmother made her daughter a handkerchief that has been passed down from oldest daughter to oldest daughter for 7 generations. I've always known that as the oldest daughter that hand embroidered lace handkerchief would be mine some day. Mom still isn't ready to give it to me, but someday it will be mine.

My father's mother loved to have toys and things for us to play with when we came to visit her as children. She created what she called "Family History in a Trunk." She had collected several pieces of clothing, scarves, hats and more from older family members. She put these all in a trunk for us to play dress up. As we played with these dresses and accessories, she would tell us who they belonged to and how they were related to us. Grandma probably had a head start on that project because her mother owned a dress shop in the town where she grew up. In fact, a trunk of dress up clothes was the perfect way for us to come to know that side of the family precisely because of the dress shop. Even though I don't remember much about which of the clothes belonged to whom, she associated me with the clothing of her forbearers and with the dress shop through the dress up clothes she kept for us.

 Guess The Heirloom Play "guess the heirloom." Do you have a unique heirloom in your family which isn't commonly used anymore? Gather your family together and play "guess the heirloom." You can play the game like 20 questions or tell whether each guess is getting warmer or colder (closer to the truth or further). Have your family guess what the item was used for and to whom it belonged.

 Heirloom Catalog Create a catalog of your heirlooms and list who will inherit each item. Working together with your family members, make a list of all the heirlooms in your family. Make sure each notation includes a description of the item, who it belonged to and where and how it was used. You can avoid hard feelings later if you decide now who will be the next person to inherit the item.

 Family History In A Trunk Create some family history in a trunk. Do you have some clothing or toys which you don't mind having handled? Pull them together to create a dress up box or toy box for the children in your family. If you don't have clothing that actually belonged to previous family members, you can collect other clothing from historical periods. Connect each piece of clothing or each toy to a story from your family's past. The children in your family can play with the items while you teach them the stories, or create skits about your family's experiences.

 Make A New Heirloom Perhaps you can work with family members to create a new heirloom for your family. Share your skills with your family by creating something that will be passed down to the next generations with woodworking, sewing, quilting, doll making or other crafting talents. Work together to create a representation of your family's history. Include something about each of your living family members to connect them closely to their ancestors.

Charts

A genealogy chart is a great messenger for your family's history. The visual representation of relationships and important dates can easily explain the overall structure and details of a family. Genealogy charts typically show some vital information (usually vital statistics) with lines between the people to show relationships. The dates and places that are usually included give the viewer a sense of how the family moved in time and geography. You can see the generations that pass from place to place and who was related to whom.

There are as many kinds of charts, large and small, as there are families. They come in circles, fans, squares, up, down and sideways. Each type of chart can enhance your research. Some show ancestors of the selected person, some show their descendants and some show conglomerations of both. They can be configured to show step families and adoptive families, cousins, aunts, uncles, in-laws and outlaws. Charts can include graphics such as maps and documents, along with narratives and family mottos. And of course, the most engaging charts include pictures of the people represented. Picture charts make the family come alive with a face, and the context of the time and place to go with it.

You may already know that I'm pretty passionate about genealogy charts. For many years, my husband and I have run Family ChartMasters and we boast that we can create any kind of chart you can dream up. We've seen people use charts in lots of different ways—usually to share family information with their family members. We feel that we are family history evangelists giving people the tools to visually engage their family members. One lady worked for months to create 7 matching charts, one for her father's family and one for each of her aunts, showing pictures for some of their ancestors and every one of their numerous descendants. She worked really hard to make sure she had a picture of each person and the charts were beautiful. She took them to her family reunion and reported back to us that there were many more attendees than ever before because everyone had come to see the charts. They gave her a standing ovation for her work and, best of all, she had several nieces and nephews ask her if she would help them learn more about their history. She told us that the original seven sisters on her charts had fought like cats and dogs. Their children had grown up with hard feelings towards each other. She said that these charts had fostered a unity that they had never seen before. Each member was an important part of the family because they were all on the charts.

Another of our favorite clients uses our charts to inspire his friends and family members about the value of their family and the nobility of their past. He works with them to discover facts about their ancestors and helps them scan their pictures. He then goes hunting for more pictures among the close relatives of his friends. He loves creating big picture charts that include the ancestors and descendants of the family. One of the recipients of his charts told him that the chart is a magnet for his grandchildren when they come for a visit. They love to find themselves on the chart and see how they fit into the wonderful family. Our client finds great satisfaction in bringing that cohesion to the families of his friends.

Creating a chart together can be a great family activity. Children can write in their names and birthdays and you can choose images together which represent your family. You might add a prominent personal quality to each person on the chart, or with ancestors you could highlight military service, countries of origin, immigrants, or images of where the family lived or a timeline of their life.

 Art Piece You can create a beautiful work of art to frame and show off in your home. Having an appealing work of art that visually expresses your family can be a conversation piece for family members and visitors alike. Many genealogy software programs are available to help you create a chart, you can draw one yourself, or you can have one professionally printed. Make sure to add the visuals that make it compelling, be that portraits or other images relevant to your family.

 Working Chart Sometimes a quick draft working chart for writing on and adding more information will do the trick. These charts can be used to record and collect information or move data off the computer screen onto a hard copy for further interpretation and new research directions. The great thing about working draft charts is that they encourage your family members to get involved and add information, and there is no better way to gather information from your living family members. There is something about putting it down on paper that makes family members grab a pencil when they see something wrong.

Sugar Cookie Chart My daughter and I found this in a *Family Fun* magazine and knew we had to try it. Each person in the family is represented by a sugar cookie decorated to look like the person. Instructions can be found at the Family Fun website (familyfun.com.) You can see our version on the August 19th 2011 post on my blog at The Chart Chick (www.thechartchick.com.) We used licorice for the relationship lines, cookies for the faces, mini M&Ms for eyes, chocolate sprinkles and frosting for hair with chocolate sprinkles for doggie fur. Needless to say, it was a hit.

Maps Hanging a world map up on the wall is a great way to encourage curiosity about your family's geographical and ethnic background. Use a marker or place pins in the countries and towns that you know your ancestors came from. String or draw lines to show immigration and see if you can illustrate how your past brought you to where you are now. Add more information to the map as you discover more about your family.

Timelines Timelines can be a great tool to place your family in the context of history as a whole. You can string a cord and attach events on paper with paper clips, or arrange items along a wall or hallway, or draw it out on a long piece of paper. Insert important events that happened in your family, and then embellish them with important events in world and local history. This can give children and adults alike a time frame on which to balance the history of their own people.

Diorama Create a representation of your family in 3D. Creating a diorama of the family homestead or some other scene in your family's history can be a fun project for younger children. A reconstruction of an immigrant scene or a military battle works well. Consider constructing a gingerbread model of an old family home. Perhaps you can multi-purpose a school project. You might try using pictures and names to create a 3D version of a genealogy chart connecting the people together to show relationships and time frames. A descendancy chart works really well as a cascading mobile.

Collage Using copies of your pictures and documents, create a collage of the images in your family's history. You may want to use glue and scissors. Or you may want to create a digital collage using your computer. Framing sets of pictures together in a single frame with a similar theme or context is effective, too. Be sure to display your work where the family can see it, ask questions, and discuss it.

You can also surround yourself with your family history by working with plants around your home, whether it be a garden plot, some planters on a porch, or just some inside plants. Those plants can be related to your family history. Do you know any of your ancestor's favorite plants or flowers? Do you know what plants they grew? Do you have any farmers in your past or do you remember the flowers in your grandparent's yard? Do you have any pictures of family houses with distinctive landscaping?

You can begin on a small scale by planting meaningful plants in and around your home. Plant markers can be used to distinguish plants and connect them to certain people in your history. Children can help care for the plants, whether smaller plantings or a whole garden. Be sure to mention to your family why the plant is associated with your family's past. Small moments like this can help infuse the identity of your family into the next generation.

My maternal grandmother's favorite flower was the lilac. When I was young, she would often try to visit us when they were in bloom because they didn't grow well where she lived. We would bring big armfuls into the house and arrange them in huge, fragrant bouquets, even in the years she wasn't able to visit. Later, when my grandparents moved closer to us, they planted a large hedge of lilacs, and my grandfather taught me about the different varieties and which were valued for smell, looks and etc. Of course, as I have been on my own, I have always loved big bouquets in my house, too. The sweetness of those memories has made them my favorite flowers. I planted one where we live now in honor of Grandma Dana.

We have planted crocuses for my mother, impatiens for Kim's mother, rose bushes for my Grandmother Carpenter, hollyhocks for Grandmother Schwendiman, tiger lilies for Grandma Anderson, and violas for Nama (whose name was Viola). The honor I have for the great legacy these women have left me is beautifully woven into our landscaping. The love, work ethic, and patience they taught me are often stretched in my gardening abilities.

When deciding on plants to incorporate in your surroundings, be sure to include only plants that will grow in your area. If you have moved to a different climate than where your family is from, it may take a little creativity to honor your ancestors with plants. Look online for growing directions and plant care hints, then choose plants that will beautify your home while you teach your family about those that came before.

 Favorite Flowers Plant some of your ancestor's favorite flowers. Were any of your grandmothers named after a flower? Do you know what their favorite perfume was or their favorite color? You might even know what flower they loved. Look in family pictures for flowers around the family home, in floral arrangements or wedding bouquets. Which of these flowers might work in your landscaping or in your home?

 Plant Markers Use plant markers with the name of your ancestors near the plants that represent them. You can purchase ready-made markers made from ceramic or metal. You can also use rocks or popsicle sticks and label them with the name of the person associated with the plant. Make sure the plants and the markers have a place of prominence so that visitors and family members will see that there is something special about those particular plants.

 Vegetables Plant some crops and vegetables. Most of us have some ancestors who were farmers. Do you know what crops they raised? Did they have a kitchen garden? Look for clues in your family's recipes. What fresh vegetables did your ancestors have? What was typically grown in the farms in their area? Did they preserve any specific type of food? Try growing a few vegetable plants in the planters around your home, or clear a space for a garden and see if you've inherited a green thumb.

 Herbs Try planting herbs for food or medicine. Before modern medicine, our ancestors relied a lot on plants for their healing properties. Do you have any family stories about using plants for medicinal purposes? What herbs were used in your ancestor's community? What herbs and spices were used in your family's recipes? An herb garden is perfect for a kitchen window sill or when space is a consideration.

Heirloom Plants Grow some heirloom vegetables or flowers. Did you know that many species of plants which our ancestors grew are harder to find today? There are organizations dedicated to maintaining antique plant species and making sure the heirloom varieties live on. Look online for heirloom plant suppliers. See if you can learn what kinds of plants may have grown in your ancestor's community. Be sure to ask about growing conditions where you live. Plant a few types of seeds and you may be able to see what your ancestor's food really tasted like or smell the floral scents they smelled.

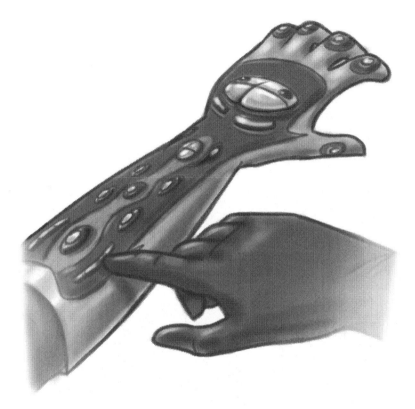

Section Three

Geek Grandma's
hi-tech gadget gloves.

Geek Grandma Knows That The Easiest Way To Plug In To Her Family Is Out On The Net.

Technology is constantly changing. There is always something new to learn and sometimes it seems hard to keep up. The historical resources available on the net have been growing and exploding at an amazing rate. New databases and archives and technologies to help you trace your family lies come online every day. If you have a family line you haven't checked online for a while, you should. You might be surprised at what's available. How can we harness all the online family history energy to help us attract the next generation to their family history?

Technology is Geek Grandma's best friend. She outfits family members with high tech super gloves that guide them through the internet towards their family history. The gloves have the buttons and gadgets that our little super heroes already love. Grandma has transformed them into super teaching tools. All of their family history is right at their fingertips. Their fingers fly across the buttons with super speed learning this and researching that. Grandma can usually learn a lot from watching how the younger generation navigates the internet. The next generation seems to have come equipped with the skills to naturally keep up with all of it.

Geek Grandma leverages the super gadgets that her children and grandchildren already use to help them understand their past. She encourages them to help her research and learn more about the family's history by surfing good family history sites on the web. She enlists their help with digitizing the family's heritage and helping other people find theirs, and she communicates often with her family via social media while expressing to them her love for their ancestors. All kinds of resources on the net are helpful to Geek Grandma when she is teaching her family the strength of their family's history.

Family history research is completely different now that it was in the past. Most people spend their free time learning about their family history in their slippers now, combing the internet for tidbits of information in the comfort of their own homes. Of course there are still many, many archives that are not digitized and one may need to travel or send away for documents that complete the family's story, but that isn't the starting point for most beginners. Youth naturally gravitate to the easy and the electric, so that's a good place to encourage their curiosity into their family's past.

When I have suggested to my teenagers that they might be interested in Ancestry's latest app, or the FamilySearch indexing tool on my ipad or smart phone, they are much more inclined to pick up on what I've suggested. Packaging their family history in the latest tech gadgets always intrigues my kids. GPS positioning and mobile mapping is great when working in cemeteries and finding family homesteads. Scanning and photographing documents is easier. Storing your information online is useful so that the family can access it. Keeping track of everything is quickly becoming effortless with helps for citations and improvements in genealogy software and apps. Forthcoming technical developments will always be interesting to our techie kids.

Keeping up on the latest developments in the genealogy world will certainly pay off for Geek Grandma. She can head into the future holding tight to her posterity secure in the knowledge that they are enlightened and strengthened by their past. Geek Grandma plugs in to her family's past and future on the net.

Curious Surfing

The pull of the surf is harsh these days. There are so many things out there to learn, so many things to be curious about. The internet is all present in our lives. It is at work, at home, at school, on our desks and in the palm of our hand. Few are the adults or children who can concentrate well on their computer tasks and not wander off into all the amazing things the internet holds conveniently close by.

This draw of the surf can be a great thing when you are learning, and what better to be learning about than your family history? A wise parent or grandparent will encourage surfing—curious research—about their family history. There are all sorts of sites to help you explore the micro history of your family. Genealogy research is huge on the internet. It is always exciting to see what the next generation can find.

When one of my sons was thirteen he became interested in my grandmother's family history research—specifically the large Personal Ancestral File computer file we inherited. I gave my son a copy and decided to let him go to town. I was pretty particular about the information I had collected at that point and I was afraid of what he would do to mess up my research so I kept my original information in a separate file. That way we wouldn't have to disagree about his research practices and he could just be curious. Cutting him loose with it turned out to be one of my best ideas. He set out on the internet and soon had us linked all the way to Adam -- and even more exciting, through the lineage of Thor. Obviously there would have to be some questions about our blood connection to a Norse Myth but he was really excited about it. Talk about an inspiring ancestor for a 13 year old boy!

My son's excitement about his discoveries was more than enough to balance out his lack of sound research practices. I had to keep reminding myself that he was a beginner, just as I had once been. Also, I had to remember that if I let him be excited now, he'll be a wonderful researcher when he is my age—as long as I don't squash his enthusiasm with the details he isn't interested in. Later, we had talks about how unreliable royal lineages are and how to properly keep track of where he finds things, but for now, his curiosity was piqued and he was on his way.

Giving a little bit of guidance about where to go to find family history resources and a starting place, then asking for help in your own research may be just the thing for your teens. Don't worry about teaching them how to do research on the net, they already know how. They will catch on to it much faster than you can, even if you are pretty tech savvy. Just stand back and watch them teach you a thing or two.

 Compiled Databases How far can you go? Check out some of the compiled databases online, Being a name collector is common for beginning family historians. It is fun to see how far you can stretch the family lineage and where it leads. Ask for help in finding new people to connect to your family tree. You can start a beginner out on a major compiled database such as FamilySearch (familysearch.org), Ancestry (ancestry.com) or another large database. Give them a few people to start their search with and see how far they can go.

 Find A Grave Find a Grave (findagrave.com) is a fun, free website where you can not only find information about your own family's past, but also help other people find information on their families. Take a look around the site for your own ancestors first, but then see if there are any requests for cemeteries in your area. Take a picnic and a camera and see if you can help out another family historian by uploading pictures from a cemetery near your home.

 Popular Websites Prompt your children to learn more about your family and their circumstances by checking some of the popular websites with historical family information. For example, look for the 1930 census that tells if the household had a radio, or the 1940 census where you can find information on the work your ancestors were doing. The Ellis Island website has information about immigrant ancestors who came through Ellis Island and the FamilySearch Wiki will teach you how to do research in the areas your family lived. Google some of the people in your family tree combined with their spouse's name or their location and see what resources pop up.

 Children's Websites There are lots of family history websites geared for kids. You can get started with the youth section in the popular search site Cyndi's List (cyndislist.com/kids). Or try out the resources collected by the print publication Family Tree Magazine (familytreemagazine.com/kids). Don't settle for a website that tries to make kids into grown up researchers. Be sure to look for the websites that make it fun. And of course check out the comprehensive list we have compiled at Zap the Grandma Gap (zapthegrandmagap.com) for all the latest and the greatest websites for kids.

Indexing and Digitizing

Another great project for children and teens is to work on an indexing or digitizing project. Taking your ancestors pictures, documents, or journals and putting them into electronic form (digitizing) allows them to be searched, backed up and easily shared. Coordinated indexing projects help create searchable databases where people can look for their ancestors. As youth are exposed to family history materials, they become accustomed to the tools genealogists use and begin to see how interesting the details of the past can be.

Indexing can be very addictive. It doesn't involve a lot of analysis and can be done in small chunks of time. There is an element of doing "just a few more" that can encourage obsessive progress on even the most daunting projects. Some parents have been delighted to find that youth who are addicted to video games can be quite attracted to indexing, something with a more lasting value than the latest game.

The 1940 census indexing project was launched in 2012 to encourage volunteers to help index the census so that it could be searched. Volunteers downloaded a census page and were guided to type in each person's name and particular details so that a database could be built for researchers to use. The organizers were surprised with the speed and enthusiasm of the amazing people who chipped in to help. The whole project was completed in only 124 days with more than 160,000 volunteers, many of them youth, processing the more than 132 million people who lived in the United States in 1940. To build on this community success, other projects have been brought online and many collections are available for volunteers to help index.

Likewise, your own family may have items that need to be digitized so that they are accessible to your family members in the electronic age. Scanned pictures and documents are useful in creating family histories, charts, blogs, websites, etc. etc. Digitizing opens up all sorts of avenues for sharing and recording your family history. Written materials such as letters and journals may likewise be digitized by typing in the information so as to create a searchable and publishable computer file. Big family projects such as these can seem overwhelming but when you collaborate with other family members, the task is easier.

Scan Pictures And Documents When pictures are digitized you can do all sorts of things with them. Scanning pictures is the first step to using them to engage your family members with their past. When collections of pictures are digitized, they are also available for future projects. Electronic versions of images can be corrected and cleaned up if there is damage, and they are crucial to sharing your history with the next generation through social media and the web.

 Digitize Journals Or Family Documents When digitizing written family documents, you will want to scan the documents first to capture any details in the writing and preserve the actual documentation, handwriting and physical characteristics of the piece. Once the images are collected it is valuable to create a typed document so that it can be searched and used in other formats. Once typed, sections of the work can be edited to create an abridged copy or parts of the work can be used in a blog, website or in another communicable form.

 Indexing Sign up at familysearch.org to participate as a volunteer indexer. You will have to download a small piece of software to help the indexing effort. Once you have signed up and downloaded the software, you can download a "batch" of documents to index. There are usually several choices of documents that you can work on. As you use the software, each field of the document will be highlighted and you simply type in the information you see. Sometimes the handwriting is hard to read, but each entry is keyed in by two people and then double checked by an arbitrator when necessary. You can watch your statistics and keep track of the progress you are making. There is a real sense of accomplishment when you can see the numbers and know you've helped other people find information about their family members.

 Society Projects Your local genealogy society most likely also has an indexing or archiving project that you can help with. Many of these projects are facilitated online similar to FamilySearch projects but they can be more localized and specific to where your family lived. You might even find your own predecessors while you are working. These smaller projects are very valuable to the genealogy community because they usually access records that are otherwise unavailable to distant family members.

Bribery Older family members who are observant see the youth in their family as a natural fit for an indexing or digitizing project since they have the technical skills necessary to accomplish the project. However, these same activities may seem overwhelming when there is a lot of work to be done. Most youth will not immediately see the value of such a task but will view it as drudgery. You may want to encourage them with payment or privileges that they can earn as sections of the project are completed. If it is your agenda to accomplish the task more than it is theirs, some form of reward should be involved. If the task is large, break it up into stepping stones that the young person can reach to maintain motivation. Don't worry though. Many hard core genealogists will tell you that they became involved because their grandparent paid them to help with their family history efforts. Engaging the next generations may take a little prompting at first, but there are big pay offs for everyone involved in the end.

Family Websites

Does your family have a website? You can create a website for a family reunion, a certain branch of the family or for your immediate family. Public family websites are great to attract cousins who are looking for their own family history, and those cousins may be able to give you more information about your common ancestors too. Some people even call family history websites "cousin bait." In addition, private websites provide an opportunity for living family members to share information about their lives in a place where private information is kept only for the family. Either way, it is great to branch out on the net and start plugging in to your family.

It may seem overwhelming to create a family website, but don't worry. You have the technological wizards you need right in your own family. Today's youth seem to come prewired with internet skills. Website creation is a perfect way to get the next generation involved in your family's heritage. It creates a gathering place for your family history while getting the youth in your family involved. Cooperation across the generations to create the website can result in stronger relationships when there is a sense of shared mission and accomplishment. As mentioned in the last chapter, if it is your priority more than theirs, you should be prepared to compensate them in some way for their efforts. Then, as the pictures and stories cross their screens, they'll become acquainted with their forbearers and you'll start to see the benefits their family history can bring to their lives.

When one of my sons was 15 years old I asked him to help me with a family history digitization project. My great-grandfather left my father his antique Amberola machine with 4 drawers of blue wax cylinders containing music and lectures from the early 1900s. We are incredibly blessed to have this amazing piece of history in my family and it even still works. When you crank up those old cylinder records, the sounds transport you back in time in a breathtaking way. I knew it would be a wonderful project to digitize these sounds so our whole family could enjoy them and learn more about the life my great-grandfather lived. My 15 year old son had the perfect technical skills that we needed. We picked a time when his school work wasn't too busy and got to work.

After recording the sounds digitally, my son took them home and processed them for me. Then, he built a far better website to house them than I could ever have, even though I have the technical skills to do it. He started with a short introduction to my great-grandfather's life. It is the perfect length to catch a family member's interest since it felt like the right amount of information to him. Then he proceeded to research the history of the Amberola machine and the cylinders that play on it. He found some interesting websites and additional history to add to our site. I helped him build a background to his specifications that matched our other projects, then he added some gadgets that will help viewers listen to the recordings. When he got engrossed in the project I was reluctant—for the first time ever—to make him stop "messing around" on the computer and go to bed.

The beauty of the whole project was the way my son came to know his great-great-grandfather. The pictures on the cylinder sleeves were from the Edison factory that created the machine, and the copyright notices were interesting examples of how Edison was trying to protect his inventions. Originally, my son was excited about being able to use something invented and created by Thomas Edison himself—a personal hero. In the process he found out that his great-great-grandfather was on the cutting edge of technology in his time; a tech geek much like my son. We came to realize he may have inherited that trait from this great-grandfather.

Private Gathering Places There are several websites where you can create a private gathering place for your family members with birthday reminders, message boards, histories and stories and, of course, the all important pictures. Check out My Heritage (myheritage.com) or My Family (myfamily.com—part of Ancestry.com) or just google "Family Website" for a list of places. On these websites, your family can safely gather online and check in with each other's lives. Sign up and you will find instructions on how to invite your family members to participate. Once your site is established, be sure to embellish it with plenty of stories and pictures of your family's past as well as your family's present.

Family Resources Website If you are experienced enough to create your own website using the resources you have about your family's history, you can register for a specific domain and host it on a web hosting service. Do you have any pictures or old letters that might make an interesting website? These are perfect subjects for the so called "cousin bait" and might even lead you to more information.

You can see our digitization project about my great-grandfather's Amberola at cadp.familychartmasters.com. Is there a treasure trove of resources in your family waiting to be digitized and brought into the modern age?

 Genealogy Software Helps You may want to put the vital statistics and other information you have gathered about your family members and their relationships on a website for other people to learn about that branch of your family tree. If you have the information you have collected in a genealogy software program such as RootsMagic (rootsmagic.com), Family Tree Builder (myheritage.com), Legacy Family Tree (legacyfamilytree.com), or Family Tree Maker (familytreemaker.com) you will be able to create a database to put on the web automatically, but you will still need to find a web hosting service to host it. You can then embellish the site with your family's stories and pictures. I have worked with some of my father's cousins to create such a website at the Joseph Hatten Carpenter family website (jhattencarpenterfamily.org). You can see resources, genealogy, pictures and information related to that part of our family. Just be careful on your website to block the private information you have on any living relatives. Even though birth and marriage dates and places are a matter of public record, some family members may not appreciate you broadcasting their data.

Photo Sharing Sites There are lots of photo sharing sites on the web where you can privately share images with other people by invitation. Flickr (flickr.com), Picasa (picasa.com), PhotoBucket (photobucket.com) and SmugMug (smugmug.com) are a few such sites. You can find others by searching for "photo sharing." Since your photos are your first and greatest ally in the quest for the next generation's interest, these sites can be really useful to share the images of your family. They will also help you disseminate the images so that the whole family can have access to them, and they will be retrievable in case of an emergency. Sign up for a free account, start scanning and invite your family to take a look. Better yet, see if your children will help you scan and upload the pictures, and then reward their efforts with a visit to the local ice cream shop.

Social Networking

Social networking can be a fantastic way to connect generations in your family—especially the youth. While some people are critical of how Web 2.0 has taken so much of our human contact from the real world to the digital world, I've found that it can break down barriers that exist when there are residual hard feelings in the family or even when you are dealing with a typical crabby teenager. Social networking is especially useful across the miles when your extended family is separated by location. When used effectively, it can even be useful when generations of your family are separated by time.

The powerful result of fusing your family history with social networking is that it hits the next generation where they live and breathe. Start with the places your family members check every morning or multiple times a day. Just use them in a family history oriented way such as including brief funny stories, interesting facts and, of course, the all important pictures. Be sure to keep posts short, vivid and eye catching to match the fast moving pace of social networking. If you can weave a little historical background into your communications with your family, you can introduce the benefits of knowing their origins as part of their daily networking ritual.

As my immediate family began to spread out across the country and throughout the world, we were concerned that we would be able to keep in touch as well as we did when we all lived near each other. We tried several avenues of communication to be able to continue to "hang out" together. We experimented with various chat programs, a private blog and a private facebook group to be able to talk with each other and sometimes share family history information. Video conferencing and email proved very useful. Even though my sisters were adults, I have had a great time shooting them an email about our grandpa's 1940 census page or a YouTube video I found about farming practices in the area our family was from. I've typed our great-grandfather's poetry into the chat feed and sent new pictures that I've found on the internet. Close family members are the best people to share my new find with because it is their history too. Some of my sisters are more family history oriented and some of them are not (yet) but we all share the same heritage, so it is a good common ground subject to talk about. We love commenting back and forth on blog and facebook posts. It continues to make me feel a part of a bigger whole and a support group that has my back. Stronger relationships have come from the work we put into communicating and staying close.

Be aware that using social networking tools to correspond with your family puts up some artificial walls and may give people the opportunity to say things that they wouldn't say in real life. That can be good and bad. Like many other parents, I was a little worried about letting my children get involved in social networking sites. Each family has to determine for themselves what the right age is to allow their children to sign up for social communication sites, but when there is a strong and active family group online, the danger for children goes down because family members can watch out for each other. When he knows that Grandma, Mom and his favorite Uncle Joe are watching, a child may behave better online than he might otherwise.

 Family Facebook Group I once heard someone say that they had created a Facebook account for their mother who had passed away in order to share the stories and pictures of her life. When friend requests were sent to her family members, one young niece responded that she felt closer to her grandmother than she ever had before and that she felt like her grandmother was "a friend." In fact, her grandmother became "her friend" in a way that this teen could relate to. By using Facebook, the family historian was speaking in a teen language. While I'm not suggesting that you create an account for a deceased person on a social networking site, you can create gathering places for your family such as a page or a group. You can design Facebook groups to be private and by invitation only if you are worried about the privacy of what you'll be posting, but I would encourage you to create a group that is public as "cousin bait." That way you may end up teaching not only your close family about their history, but possibly even communicating with more extended family that you have yet to meet. Post stories, interesting documents and pictures so that they come up in the news feed of family members. Be sure to like the zapthegrandmagap group on Facebook for more great ideas about how to use family history.

 Twitter Feeds There are many great examples of how to use Twitter in a historical way. You can follow museums, publications, random fact feeds, even tweets of witty historical sayings and eclectic events. There are lots of genealogy Twitter feeds too, sometimes pertaining to a geographical area or a family line. Follow a few and you can get a feel for what you might be able to do with your own history. You could tweet "a day in the life," or a fact about "my ancestor." Be aware that anyone can follow a Twitter feed and read anything you've written at any time. There is no private aspect to Twitter. Be sure to follow @zapgrandmagap for more great ideas about how to bridge the generations with your family history.

 Blogs Genealogy blogging is a large and growing phenomenon with thousands of genealogy bloggers telling the story of their families. In fact, the geneablogger community is a fun community that you can interact with through other social networking sites and the Geneabloggers website (geneabloggers.com). Genabloggers help each other with weekly and daily prompts to inspire ideas about family stories you can write. You can also search the web for "personal history prompts" that will give you some ideas. Blogging is a great way to record your history in little chunks while sharing it with others and building a great collection for future generations to use as a foundation to their identity. And, of course, the blog at zapthegrandmagap.blogspot.com will give you more ideas about blogging.

 Email Newsletter Good old fashioned email is a solid, easy way to present information about your ancestors. Most everyone checks their email consistently. Keep your emails short so they don't get ignored in the rush of communication. You could offer your family a question a week with a prize for the person who knows the answer. You could share a story. I periodically send my family "Hey have you seen this?" emails with new items I've found about our history. With larger family organizations you might want to subscribe to an email newsletter service that helps you design emails in html and include graphics and formatting. Be considerate about the recipient's time and don't fill their inbox too often, but give them a taste now and then. See if you can inspire questions in a reply email. Check zapthegrandmagap.com for a great newsletter offer that will help you strengthen your family ties and get you thinking about how to more effectively use email with your family.

 YouTube Video is one of the most attractive tools you can use to inform your family about their family history. YouTube has it exactly right with their small clips that work for short modern attention spans. You can convert old or current family videos, narrate pictures, show instructions for family recipes or demonstrate family traditions. Combine your YouTube videos with the social networking options above by emailing and tweeting your latest video or posting it to your Facebook group. Combining resources will give you the winning combination that will be sure to attract your family's attention. Check out the social networking links at zapthegrandmagap.com to try out all of these social networking ideas.

Surnames

Another avenue for involving the whole family in the past is to encourage exploring family names and surnames. Rather than looking for information about your particular pedigree, are there interesting aspects to the names in your family's past? Surrounding the individual stories in your family history are the larger family organizations and ancient history of the names in your family. Some youth will be interested to find out about the meanings of the names in your family tree and possible crests or heraldry relating to your family's history. This kind of inquiry isn't necessarily connected to the ancestors you know, but rather learning about the cultural and historical sources surrounding your family's name. Don't forget that there are many, many surnames in your family tree, with marriages uniting families from differing circumstances. Scope out the history of some of those patrilineal and matrilineal names and you may find some interesting aspects to your history that you hadn't imagined.

For example, the surname my husband's family brought from Czechoslovakia was Hovorka. In Czech the word means "one who talks too much." It comes from the word "Hovor" which means to talk or converse. Many family members and friends have been amused that I married into that name since I am well known for talking too much. Not only does it give me the feeling that my husband and I were meant for each other, it also makes me extremely curious about who the first person was with that name. How did that person come to be known by that name and why was it appropriate for him? How have people down through those family lines lived up to the name? Where have their descendants taken the name?

According to the sources my great-grandfather used, my maiden name Carpenter was not established the way you might think it would have been. Apparently it came from a warrior who was so effective with his sword, smiting people over the head like with a hammer, that he was given the French name "Carpentier." That information gives the name that I've lived with my whole life a different twist than I had originally supposed—and yet our Carpenter family crest has a snail in it. How could those images have come together? You might find a similarly intriguing story in your name's past as well.

You might consider joining a family organization to continue learning about your family and where they have been found throughout the world. Many people begin to probe this type of analysis when they get stuck and unable to find more information about their particular ancestors. They gather information on everyone known by that name to see if they can find breakthroughs in their own research. Some become experts on the way the name has been used and how the family has evolved through time. You may find such an alternate avenue into your family's past to be exciting.

 Name Studies To study the history and scope of a name, you might start with an organization such as The Guild of One Name Studies (www.one-name.org). These organizations serve as a place for people who are interested in a particular name to collaborate and collect information on that name. Are there any exciting or famous people who have the same surname? Could they be related? What else can you find out about people who have the same surname as yours?

 Meanings Do any of your names have an internal meaning in your language or in another language? Do these give any clues about where your family is from or how you are related to any other groups of people? What about the first names of your ancestors? Are there any names that give insight into what those people were like, or the hopes and dreams of their parents? What do you know about how names were given in your family? Are there any naming patterns, such as naming the first son with the mother's maiden name, or naming the first child after the paternal parents? What do these names tell you about your family history?

 Heraldry Are there any coats of arms or family crests related to your family's names? What can you find out about the symbols or colors used in the crest? How was the coat of arms awarded and to whom? What does this tell you about your family's history and about the area where they originated?

 Family Organizations Are there any family organizations that you might associate with to find more information about your family name? Similar to an extended family reunion organization, there are groups who encourage association among members of a family, irrespective of how distantly their pedigrees are connected.

Do these organizations have any resources about your family? What can you learn about family qualities or other attributes that might relate to your own history?

Section Four

Gifted Grandma's
Useful Utility Belt

Gifted Grandma Uses Her Creations To Teach Her Family About Their Past.

You may have family members who think history is boring. Ugh. The "b" word. They just don't want to spend time on all that dusty stuff. If your family is feeling that way, you just haven't connected them to the past by making it fun. You can make it entertaining by utilizing the right tools. Don't let anyone tell you that family history isn't interesting, because it is. If you aren't having fun yet, relax, enjoy yourself, and try out some of the activities in this chapter.

Gifted Grandma has some surprises in store for her descendants when it comes to teaching them about their family's history. She has created for them a super utility belt full of gadgets, gizmos and games galore. Her family history tools can entertain and educate at the same time. When she looks at the world in a family history way, she can see all sorts of learning tools and crafts that can be applied to connecting with her family. She makes the past fun so it is much easier to help her family realize the benefits of their history.

Some of the contraptions on Grandma's belt include books and scrapbooks about her family's history that are inviting and beautiful, games and workbooks to defeat the evils of apathy and indifference, and calendars and time capsules that reach into the future while preserving the past. She strengthens future generations by teaching them to record their feelings and experiences now and value the present as it affects generations to come. And our Grandma is truly gifted when it comes to gift giving.

She imparts important gifts that nourish her family's individual feelings of worth. Not only does she create these gifts for her family, she helps her family create their own items as well. Family history really is the ultimate gift. It is a secure foundation on which they can build their own lives and the next generations.

The tool belt I received from my family comes in handy when I am teaching my children about their history. It has taken some time to amass the tools I now have but they have been worth every effort. We have scrapbooks and quilts, children's picture books and paper dolls and bingo games. We capture my children's attention with calendars, and puzzles and journals. All sorts of craft tools and activities can be tweaked to apply to our past. I utilize all of these gadgets to help me be a better mother. They strengthen my identity and fortify my children at the same time.

One of the tools my mother gave me is the gift of family cuisine. When I was married, my mom gave me a collection of my maternal grandmother's casserole recipes. Some of them are very different than the way we cook today and add a welcome change to our usual menus when I use them. One of my favorites, because it is so different, is Raviola Casserole:

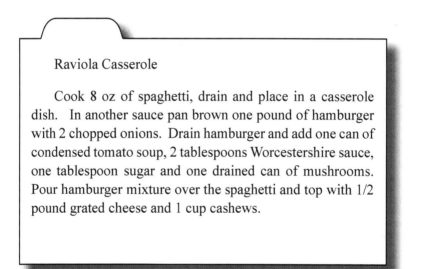

Raviola Casserole

Cook 8 oz of spaghetti, drain and place in a casserole dish. In another sauce pan brown one pound of hamburger with 2 chopped onions. Drain hamburger and add one can of condensed tomato soup, 2 tablespoons Worcestershire sauce, one tablespoon sugar and one drained can of mushrooms. Pour hamburger mixture over the spaghetti and top with 1/2 pound grated cheese and 1 cup cashews.

Who would have thought to put cashews in a recipe like this? Mmmm, simple and yummy. Bake in a 350 degree oven for 20 minutes and serve.

I've treasured the recipe cards my mother made for me. They are in her handwriting. Recently I discovered that my mother has recipe cards written in her mother's and her grandmother's handwriting. As soon as I make copies of them, I plan to add a few of my own recipes and pass them down to my daughter.

Gifted Grandma's children and grandchildren use their utility belts to spring into action when things are getting dull. There are gadgets that can transport her descendants back in time to get to know their ancestors. These gizmos pull her children close as she spends time playing with them, working alongside them, and teaching them about their roots. She utilizes every talent she has in support of her family. and every apparatus on that tool belt becomes an important part of empowering her family when it is infused with family history. The following ideas can help you get the job done in your family too.

Books and Scrapbooks

Processing and putting the information about your family's history into an accessible book format will help your descendants learn about their ancestors better than if the information is kept in file cabinets and shoe boxes. A compiled book or scrapbook about your history will help synthesize and preserve the information better. If you have a child or grandchild who is old enough, they may be able to help. You could even make copies of your photos and let the child go about creating a book of their own.

I spent hours and hours as a child looking at my parent's wedding album, their high school yearbooks, the books we have about our ancestors and my sisters' and my baby books. It was fascinating to me that there was life before I came along. I was proud of their accomplishments and developed a sense of what was expected of me as I went through those same growing up years. And, of course, any child is fascinated with pictures of themselves. As my sisters and I have grown up, my mother has kept all the pictures of our childhoods in scrapbooks. They aren't particularly decorative, but they are labeled and organized. Mom probably doesn't realize how much I picked them up and looked at them as a kid. I know that visual history of my family very well and it gave me a real sense of the passing of time in our family.

There are many crafting resources for creating beautifully decorative scrapbooks. You can also create digital picture books or full fledged family histories. There are a myriad of options available online or through print and photo retailers to assist you in publishing a book. You can also copy your books yourself by simply using your own printer and three ring binders or other office supplies. Just remember, the more attractive the book is, the more it will be picked up and read. Make sure you use lots of eye catching pictures or illustrate the book with your own drawings. Better yet, let your child or grandchild illustrate the book for you.

My Mom and I and several of my sisters have worked together to create scrapbooks about the various parts of our lives. It started as a fun, Saturday night get-together. At times, creating scrapbooks was a common ground that brought us together even when we weren't as close in other aspects of our lives. Going through the pictures and reminiscing gave us lots to talk about. Along with the time we spent together, we produced a tangible, lasting history of the family.

Your recent family pictures are probably digital and stored on a computer or digital drive where they are not accessible to the children in your family. Simple photo books or small albums with pictures in them can serve as a great reminder of a child's identity and their place in the world. Make sure that your recent family pictures are available to your children and grandchildren, even if they are only used as a screen saver for your computer.

 Short Children's Books After my mother recorded and published the oral histories of the ancestors she knew best, she also used the information she had to create shorter children's books. She has written 10-15 page books about several of my individual ancestors and for each ancestor she focused on an attribute they exhibited in their life. My great-grandparents who lived through the depression have books with the subtitles, "The Power of Sacrifice" and "The Power of Hard Work." My handcart pioneer ancestor's book focuses on "The Power of Perseverance." Each of the books has a page on the family of origin of that ancestor, a page on their early life, a page on their young adult life, a page on courtship, a page on their adult life, and a pedigree chart, etc. Mom even wrote one about how she and my dad met and Dad wrote one about each of his parents, too. These books are all beautifully bound in hard copy and every other page is illustrated with photographs or drawings. While these short children's books are probably aimed at the younger set, they are good for someone of any age with a short attention span. The more illustrations and pictures a book has, the more it pulls you into the topic. I've often thought that if I could only save one item in a fire, these books would be what I would grab.

 Kids Illustrate Your Book Perhaps the children in your family can provide illustrations for your book. My younger sisters got to illustrate one of the children's books that my mother wrote. With one great-great-grandmother, there was only one photograph of her to use in the book, but that didn't slow my mother down. She had my little sisters draw pictures of the church where the grandmother was christened (gleaned from a photo on the internet), the ship on which she immigrated to America, and the way she crossed the plains as a pioneer. Even though they weren't completely enthused about the project at the time, they got to know the stories intimately because of the research that went into creating illustrations for the book. For me, the book is all the more special because they have my sisters' drawings in them.

What Happened When While you are compiling a book, keep in mind that the story doesn't have to encompass a huge part of your family's history. It may just be a small story presented as a smaller publication. Perhaps there is a story about the trouble Grandpa got into with his brothers, or perhaps you can capture what life was like at the same age as the child you are working to involve. Think about the exciting stories in your family's past and picture them as a children's story book. How would you tell that story so that it would be interesting to read aloud?

Collections Of Letters Many families have been separated by war, economics and immigration. If so, there are probably letters that went back and forth. If you have any letters like this in your family, why not publish them so that your family members can learn about those people? A collection of letters teaches about the events that were going on in the family members' lives but also shows what the writer's personality was like and tells about the relationship between the writer and the receiver. Love letters and other letters can present a compelling narrative about your family's past. The personal narrative of a letter is a wonderful primary source—by the person, at the time—that can really bring an ancestor's thoughts and feelings to life.

Give Children Copies One of my earliest real family history encounters was with a book that I was given about my great-grandfather. My father's father wrote a short book about his father and when each of his descendants were given a copy, I received one even though I was only 10 years old. It came to live on the little white bookshelf in my bedroom. Late at night in the quiet of my room, I would pull out the book and read about my patriarchal line. I felt very close to my great-grandfather through this book. Even though my grandfather was a college professor and wrote many other important publications, this is to me, far and away, the greatest work of his life. It is the only piece of his life's work that was specifically directed at me.

I doubt my grandfather knew what an impact his decision would have to give a 10 year old granddaughter a copy of his book. He could have easily thought that I was too young to appreciate it or take good care of it, but throughout my life, I've identified with my grandfather's father very well and thus I've ultimately put a large part of my genealogy focus on his lines. My grandfather made his father come alive for me even though my great-grandfather died several years before I was born.

 Archival Scrapbooks Be sure to use archival materials in your scrapbook creations. Mount your photos on acid free, lignin free paper with photo corners and store them in albums in polypropylene or polyester (mylar) sleeves. If you keep your pictures in regular binders, a table runner placed across the top of the shelf can protect light and dust from permeating the tops of the pages. Better yet, look for binders that close completely like a box, thus protecting further from light and dust. In addition, with your most important pictures, be sure to alleviate as much uneven pressure as you can by avoiding the buttons and other 3-D doodads popular in scrapbooking. Using these will cause an ugly button indentation on the picture on the opposite page. Of course you can use cute decorations, but only in fun scrapbook projects with your extra photo copies, not with archival photographs which have no duplicates.

Games

Everyone knows that the way to make anything more fun is to make a game out of it. Family history can be fun and games too. Word games, card games, puzzle games and board games all make family history come alive. When you create family history oriented games, not only are you teaching your family about their past, you are giving them opportunities to spend quality time with you and other living family members. Games are the perfect way to connect to the past while you are connecting to each other in the present.

Ideally, you may be able to find some games that your ancestors played. Historic games like Cat's Cradle, checkers, jump rope, hopscotch, marbles and jacks are just as fun now as they were when children of past generations played them. What games come from the areas where your ancestors lived? Perhaps games or rhymes have been passed down in your family or they are mentioned in letters or in journals. It is very likely that if your ancestors enjoyed a certain game, you and your children will have fun playing it too.

"Graces" was a popular game played in the 18th and 19th century to teach young women to be graceful. Each player is given two sticks about 18 inches long. By crossing the sticks and then spreading them quickly apart, the player is able to launch a small hoop into the air for the other player to receive. The other player catches the hoop and then returns it back to the first player in a game of catch. My children and I learned to play the game of graces while we were volunteering at our local living history site. We had a great time playing catch the way our ancestors did years ago. We also learned to walk on stilts and to keep a very large hoop rolling along the ground using a stick. Recently, I taught people to play the game Cat's Cradle in a couple of situations where the participants were enthralled with how the yarn works to create shapes. Young and old alike were drawn into the fun. These were entertaining games to learn today just as they were entertaining games in generations before us.

My mother-in-law told us in her oral history that she enjoyed taking the Sears and Roebuck catalog and making paper dolls. She spent hours and hours making up stories and creating scenes with the dolls she made. Likewise my daughter, when she was young, spent many hours drawing dolls and painstakingly cutting out their dresses with little tabs to fold in back to keep the paper dresses attached to the doll. We enjoyed the activity together and created lots of little dolls to play with. If I had been a little wiser I would have employed some of our dolls to tell my daughter the story of her grandmother, but my daughter does know about her grandmother's love of paper dolls. In fact, though my mother-in-law died before my daughter was born, I think I know where my daughter got that affinity and I think her grandmother may have been smiling down at her from the heavens as she played with her paper dolls.

Look at the games your children already enjoy. Are there any family history aspects that can be brought to play? Often the key to immersing your family in their family history is to bring family history to something your family members already enjoy. Many activities just need a few details added to become a tool that teaches your children more about their family's background. Most likely, you already have all the tools right around you that you need to make family history fun.

 Workbooks, Dot To Dot, Mazes, Coloring, And Crossword Puzzles For a family reunion or a special gift, create a workbook out of your family history's stories. Dot to dots, mazes, coloring pages and crossword puzzles make great avenues for teaching about your family history. If you don't have the artistic skills to be able to pull some fun drawing games together, ask the people around you to do it.

 Paper Dolls Do you have a granddaughter or daughter interested in fashion? Try creating some paper dolls of your ancestors. You or your child can draw the dolls and the clothes, then color them, cut them out and play with them together. Instead, you might purchase a book of paper dolls and then tell stories of what happened to your ancestors with them. Pass down every detail you know about your stories and even create accessories for the paper dolls as heirlooms or props.

 Puzzles From Pictures Or Pedigree Charts Can you create a picture puzzle? With a duplicate copy of an important picture, create a puzzle for the youth in your family. You can do it yourself with heavy cardboard paper or send it to a company on the internet that creates puzzles from pictures. A pedigree chart makes a great puzzle too. You can cut it into puzzle shapes and your family will learn more about their ancestors by piecing it back together.

 Bingo, Matching Cards, Memory And Go Fish You can easily create playing cards relating to your family history. Include pictures, names, places, personality qualities, and pairs of older pictures and younger pictures of the same person, then gather the kids and play. If you can group your family in sets of four—by generation, or by lineage, creating pairs with spouses or with parents and children, then you can play just about any card game with your family history cards.

 Other Games Virtually any game can be adapted to family history with a little bit of imagination. A family event might be enhanced with a game of Jeopardy. You could use different family lines as subject headings, specific time periods or titles such as health, places, hobbies, physical characteristics, emigrants, etc. You can look for places or names in a Boggle game or Scrabble. If you can collect questions and answers you can create a Trivial Pursuit game using your regular game board and pieces but substituting your family history questions for the game's questions. Likewise, family stories can make for a fun and funny Pictionary or Charades game. Just think about the games your family likes to play and then give them a historical twist.

Calendars

A child must have a sound understanding of time and the way it moves through our lives to become an observer of generations. For young children, time can be a hard concept. It is hard to imagine that your mother had a mother and a mother before her until you have a little time under your belt and are able to see the people around you becoming older. One of the great lessons of family history is gaining a perspective of time and especially of how one generation's choices affect the generations after that.

One aspect of the march of time in a family can be illustrated with a family calendar. When you mark the seasons, anniversaries and birthdays you feel time moving and it seems that life is a little more deliberate. Timelines are an important part of genealogy and a calendar can introduce that concept to young children. They are great communication tools for the family and can serve as reminders for the family's unifying celebrations.

Especially after I left home, Mom made sure I had a calendar on my wall that had family history dates on it. I don't think I noticed the calendars much when I lived at home, but I treasure them now. The latest versions have been decorated with the photos of me and my sisters and our families through the previous year. The calendar is a great Christmas gift that now teaches my children about their extended family—aunts and uncles and cousins—in a very graphic and timely way. It creates unity among us and helps everyone remember to call each other for birthdays, anniversaries, etc. Past versions of the calendar have included family history dates, birthdays, anniversaries and more.

A calendar can be a central organizational tool for the modern family. Schedules for the family can be coordinated and family planning meetings can be organized with it. Calendars are a great way to share family pictures where everyone will see them all the time. After the calendar is used, it can actually become a journal of what happened over the past year and can be archived as a keepsake of the family's activities. A calendar can become even more of a journal when more notations are made on it. For several years when my children were babies and toddlers, I made notes on the calendar each day of the cute things they did and said. Those calendars are now precious mementos of those days when my children were small.

You can create your own calendar by cutting and pasting pictures onto a calendar with scrapbooking supplies, or create it on your computer with a word document or drawing program, or you can take it to a print shop or an online calendar creation site. You will need pictures that will show on top of each month in the calendar and you can use pictures for each day that your family has an anniversary or birthday. Ample space for pictures will help you utilize the greatest tool you have in your family history—the pictures. Wrap the calendars up for everyone as gifts and you are all set to help your family learn more about their family's history in the coming year.

Current Family Pictures Calendars can pull the extended modern family closer together with pictures of what everyone did over the past year. Collect pictures from the family taken on holidays, on vacations and throughout the summer. Use pictures from each month of the previous year to illustrate the same month in the coming year. Make sure that all family members are equally represented and then make sure family members receive copies of the calendar.

Pictures At A Certain Age Calendars can be decorated with photos from a certain time in your family. Try putting everyone's pictures on their birthdays when they were teenagers or when they were babies. Create a timeline of your family with a display of all the wedding pictures you have or all the family group pictures. Perhaps a family reunion can be memorialized each year by creating a collage of older family reunion pictures. Create a calendar using collections of pictures where family resemblances are prominent and relationships can be strengthened.

Ancestor Pictures Do you have enough pictures of your ancestors to create a calendar of just ancestor pictures? Place pictures in each month by family line or by generation, birthday or time period. Be sure to include notations about who is in the pictures and how they are related to the family. Include the dates and places the photos were taken, too, if you can.

Anniversaries Of course all anniversaries of birthdays, marriage dates and death dates should be included in the calendar. You can color code the notations according to which family line they come from. These notations are great reminders for celebrating an ancestor's birthday and sending cards and/or gifts to living family members. Include extended family members as well as ancestors and close family members. You can also include addresses, emails and phone numbers for living family members on a page in the back. Make sure you have permission from all family members to include their personal information, and then you have a great tool for helping everyone keep in touch.

Time Capsule

A time capsule is a great way to send yourself and your family members into the future. It is hard to remember in our day-to-day lives how transitory life is and how much things change from year to year and beyond. The things you see, thoughts you think and feelings you feel will be gone more quickly than you realize unless you take the time to preserve them. A time capsule is a great way to capture a moment in your family's life and send it into the future to teach future generations about who you are now.

Children tend to think only in the here and now. One of the great benefits of family history is the broad perspective it gives. When a child spends time thinking about what they will put into a time capsule to send into the future it makes them think about their future family and what life will be like at a later time. A time capsule can contain writings, artifacts, documents and anything else that will express what is important to you now. A great way to start the discussion about a time capsule is to share with the child any artifacts or heirlooms you have from your family's past. As you talk to them about the family's past and future you can instill in them how important their life is to the generations that will come after them.

When I was a senior in high school, one of my girlfriends gathered our friends together to have a special dinner and create a time capsule. We filled out sheets for our five year reunion and our ten year reunion about what we thought our lives would be like and what we wanted to accomplish. When we gathered together to open our letters to our future selves, not only were we able to reestablish old friendships and connect to each other again, but we were also able to connect to our past and evaluate what life had become. It was really fun to look back and see how much we'd grown and changed.

Like many people, our family always takes time for reflection around the holidays and especially at the New Year. We write down what we are thankful for and what our hopes and goals are for the coming year. We have a special box where we keep these thoughts and feelings. It is put away with the holiday decorations until the coming year. At the end of the year, when the decorations come back out, we hold a special meeting where we evaluate what we've accomplished and what we would like to have happen in the future. These letters to our future selves are great for self evaluation and self reflection and serve as a mechanism for setting goals and reaching for a better life. We've even saved them as a record of our thoughts and feelings throughout the years.

A time capsule can be as elaborate as an archival container or as simple as a shoebox under the bed. The best place for a time capsule is in the living area of your home. The temperatures and humidity that are best for you are also best for your time capsule. Many an artifact has been ruined by burying the item where humidity and water leaking through a foundation stone damaged it. To be a time capsule, your collection doesn't need to be hidden away, it only needs to remain closed and valued. As long as family members know where it is and when it is to be opened, a time capsule can take any form.

 Individual Time Capsules Help each family member create their own time capsule. Each family member might write a letter to their future self or a future child and carefully select items to be placed with it. You can supply each family member with a special container of their own and collect them back to be saved together, or let each family member put their own in a low traffic area such as under the bed or at the back of a closet. Designate a time for the capsule to be opened and clearly label the container with the date and the name of the person whose capsule it is.

 Favorites Create a collection of favorite items to send to your future self or to future generations. Describe each item and why it was selected for this mission. Be sure to include only items that can be left untouched for the designated period of time. A favorite toy collection that the child has grown too old for might be good for this application. If it had been a really treasured collection, such as baseball cards or matchbox cars, adulthood will bring a whole new appreciation and love for the items.

 Special Events Commemorate a special occasion with a time capsule. Weddings or births are a great time to archive some important items for the future. Designate another special occasion for the time capsule to be opened. When feelings and hopes for the future are preserved they become an important record of memories that are all too quickly forgotten.

 Cedar Chests Women of previous generations were sometimes known to have a cedar chest or hope chest that served a purpose somewhat similar to a time capsule. A young woman was encouraged to collect items such as linens, clothing and baby items in the hope chest for her future married life. Once she was married, mementos of her new life were kept in the cedar chest. The cedar in this type of chest was originally used to protect fabric but the chest can hold other items as well. Any kind of chest can serve the purpose. Old steamer trunks also make great containers. If you have inherited a steamer trunk from your ancestors, this use could be the perfect fusion of the past and the future.

Recording Their Lives

Much could be said about the value of keeping a journal. Not only does keeping a journal help you record and preserve the details of your life and your feelings, it also helps you process what is going on around you and deal with your emotions in a healthy way. Additionally journals and diaries—by the person at the time—are the ultimate primary source for historians. They are the best way to preserve yourself for the future and to get to know someone in the past.

Anyone who has access to a journal written by an ancestor knows the value of keeping a record of your life. What a treasure it is to be able to learn more about a person from their writings over a period of time, which is far more significant than one piece of writing expressing how someone feels during one time period. A valuable ancestral journal might even clearly show why the decisions were made that affected your life and where your family is now. One of the ancestors that I relate to the most kept a journal almost every day from 1884 to 1961. He wrote about his immigration to the United States, his travel to other countries, the birth of his children, the death of his wife, and even the day John F Kennedy was shot, etc. As I have read through these journals, I have come to know this grandfather, his family, their trials and their successes in an intimate way. In fact I relate most to this branch of my family tree precisely because of these journals and the impact they have made on me.

A journal can be any collection of writings. It can be a three ring binder, a leather bound volume, a sketchbook (including drawings) or a computer file. Blogs make nice journals and there are also other journaling softwares and apps that can help you record your life. Make sure if your journal is electronic that you back it up regularly. Journals can be private, where you speak your mind without worry of others reading what you think, or you can share your journal with others. You can record what happens to you and how you feel about things. You can include drawings and clippings from other sources. You can write in it daily, weekly, monthly, or whenever the mood strikes. However you record your life, it will be a great value to you and to your posterity to capture what you are thinking and feeling now.

After my divorce, I was encouraged to keep a journal. I took that advice very seriously during that period of my life. I hoped to turn the pain I was feeling into a growing experience and I knew that keeping a journal would help me process what I was experiencing. In the two journals I filled over the course of that next year, I poured my soul out about the hurt I felt, what I had learned and where I wanted to go next in my life. Later, when I married again, I decided to let my husband read those journals. He came to know firsthand what I'd been through and how those events had transpired in my life. When they are old enough, my children and even my grandchildren will read them and come to understand me and know one of the trials I conquered in my life.

Many famous people have kept a journal. The Diary of Anne Frank is a journal written by an unassuming school girl, but it has become an important part of school curriculums all over the world. If you have an ancestor who lived through a major challenge or accomplished something great wouldn't it be wonderful to have the journal they kept of their life? Keeping a journal yourself, and encouraging your children and grandchildren to keep a journal, can be a valuable family history activity that will benefit this generation and those to come.

Keep It Short A journal doesn't have to be a huge project. Writing in it can be sporadic and centered on a short topic. For example, record a day in your life, your feelings about an event or milestone, a map of your neighborhood, a timeline of your life, a list of addresses where you have lived or the floor plan of a house. For a free .pdf that the youth in your family can use to start recording their lives, go to www.zapthegrandmagap.com/downloads and print the document "MyTimeMachine.pdf." It will help them begin to record their thoughts and feelings about the life they are living now. No matter how much they write, it will be a treasure in the years to come.

Reflective Letters In journal writing, a letter can be written to future generations. At the birth of a child, a wedding, or just on a normal day, you can write a letter to a particular child telling them what you love about them and what your desires are for their future. In like manner, a general letter can be written to your future descendants, summarizing what you would like them to know about you and what your hopes are for the future. A similar letter could be written to an ancestor, or a family of ancestors, discussing with them what you have learned from their lives and how your life was affected by theirs.

 Statements Of Faith Or Belief When my father retired, he took a few days and wrote down ten specific statements of the values he felt were important to him. He called them "This I Believe." He wanted his children and grandchildren to know what beliefs guided his life. He knew that the only way his family would remember would be if he wrote them down and gave everyone a copy so that they could keep them and read them. The statement he wrote is now a treasured part of his legacy to me and my family.

 Journal Or Diary A journal or a diary makes a great gift for a child or grandchild. Keeping a journal helps a child think through what is going on in his life. Include a letter with the journal that encourages them to value the present part of their life and make good choices for the future. You might think of a special reward they could earn for writing in the journal on a regular basis. Encouraging good journal keeping will help children learn to write and express themselves in a way that will benefit them throughout their lives.

 Parent's Or Grandparent's Journal A mother's, father's, grandmother's or grandfather's journal about the cute things the children do can be a source of great self-esteem and pride to a young child. A record of the parent's and grandparent's love and concern for the child can be such a great comfort, whether now or in future years, when the child receives the journal. Try writing about the choices you are making and the struggles you have in trying to help the children become the best they can be. If there are multiple children, you could write short sections in a journal for each child, or write in one journal and plan to make copies for each of the children. Be sure to record your feelings on special occasions and your pride in their accomplishments. Whenever you choose to share this journal with your child it will be a great treasure.

Gifts

When gift giving occasions come around, most children really don't need another gadget or toy. What gifts can you give to strengthen self esteem and pull them closer to their family? Especially as youth get older, and at special occasions such as weddings or baby showers, a family history oriented gift can be the perfect thing to express your faith in them and in their future.

Many of the ideas in this book and in this chapter can be used as family history gifts. Charts, books, journals, games, calendars, time capsules and etc. all make good gifts. Choose something that will resonate with the child's interests. You might want to include your children and grandchildren in creating a special family history gift for someone else. Your gift will be all the more meaningful because of the multi-generational contributions.

My family has often exchanged gifts of family history. In fact, my parents have requested that rather than purchase another gadget for them, we choose a service project or family history project for their gifts. Recently my children and I decided to digitize some of our family's history as a service project to give my mom and dad for Christmas. It was a huge extraction project that was long and hard for a couple of teenagers, but they cooperated largely because it was a gift for my parents. My children knew how impressed their grandparents would be that we had accomplished such a large amount of work and they worked hard because they have a good relationship with my parents. It was really gratifying to see them proud of the work they had done, and to have my parents so pleased with the results.

Other gifts my family has exchanged include collections of family history pictures that my dad has helped digitize, collections of stories, antique jewelry and other simple family heirlooms. Creating or researching a family history project as a gift is a great way to complete a project because of the natural deadline it creates. You have to finish the project for the gift giving occasion. Creating a family history gift can make a busy time even more busy, but it does ensure that the project is finished. I don't know if my parents knew that requesting family history gifts instead of other presents would create deadlines for us, but it works and has worked well as I've gotten my teenagers involved, too.

Birthdays, weddings, anniversaries and holidays are even more special when a gift honors your heritage and binds the family closer together. Especially as family members get older, family history gifts become more meaningful. They are a great way to honor older family members with something that really matters. At Family ChartMasters we often create pedigree art pieces for wedding anniversaries and milestone birthdays. The visual depiction of a family is a beautiful way to celebrate someone who has dedicated their life to raising their family. We often hear back that the chart is a very moving memento for the recipient.

 Meaningful Moments An important occasion can be the perfect time to give a gift of family history. Baby showers, milestone birthdays, wedding or anniversary presents are particularly meaningful because of the important nature of the event. A family history chart showing the combination of the two families coming together in marriage could be most appropriate as a couple begins their life together. An heirloom of a baby toy or a christening gown from a previous generation can be a treasured gift to the new mother. Such items, presented at such important moments, tie generations together at a time when emotions are strong. Such a gift can be a deeply meaningful expression of love to the recipient.

 Recipes Every Christmas my mother makes honey candy for the family from the recipe her great-grandmother used. It is a treasured tradition that I know will continue on in the next generations because we all love it and look forward to it every year. We often get together to make the candy and Mom has made sure that we all know how to make the tricky recipe. The kids help stretch the candy and, of course, every one helps eat it. Perhaps you have a recipe or a collection of recipes you can pass down or make for gifts. If you make the food as a gift, make sure the recipient gets the recipe, too, so that they can continue to pass the recipe into the next generation.

 Heirlooms Do you have any family heirlooms that you would like to pass down? Consider giving them to the next generation now rather than waiting until later. If you have children who are old enough to take care of an historic item from your family, and if you feel that they understand the value of your family's history, consider giving the heirloom to the child as a special gift. Make the presentation of the item a statement of your faith in them and the future. Distributing heirlooms among the family now will help avoid frustrations later when you have passed on.

 Digitizing Perhaps you could digitize items from your family's history and distribute them to family members. A few years ago, one of my sisters, with the help of another sister and her husband, created a DVD of photos and music from the time our parents met until the present time. It's a powerful reminder of the good times and love we've shared as a family. Copies can easily be made and distributed as our families grow. Mom and Dad still can't watch it without getting teary-eyed. It is amazing how that perspective allows us to see the good in our past and forget about the struggles common to any family.

 Collections, Projects, Crafts Perhaps you can make a creative display of your family's history as a holiday gift. A family history quilt, or wall hanging, a chart or collage, or craft items can be tweaked to include a little background on the family. Use copies of any important documents or pictures—keep originals stored away where they are safe for the future. Take a trip to your local craft store with your family history in mind and let your imagination start churning. You are bound to come up with something that will be a future family heirloom.

 Family History Gifts Ask for family history instead of gifts. For Mother's Day each year, Mom has asked us not to give her presents, but rather to give her a scrapbook page of a positive childhood memory. These pages have been combined in a book that has become much more meaningful than anything else we could have given her. On their wedding anniversary one year, I borrowed my parents' wedding album and, using fabric transfers, created a quilt of all their wedding pictures. While it was a lot of work, it was fun to create something for them that I knew they would love so much.

Section Five

Groovy Grandma's
Vivid Virtual Helmet

Groovy Grandma Uses The History Around Her Family's Past To Make Their Progenitors Come Alive

What if the information you have about your family's past life is really sporadic? It's hard to get excited about family history when the information is sparse. How do you tell the story of your ancestors with the details and colors that make it interesting? Even if you know a lot about your family's history, how do you really make those people come to life? How can your children and grandchildren really get to know them?

Groovy Grandma has the answer—virtual helmets. Our little superheroes are good at getting into the bygone groove. They use the virtual helmets of historical context Groovy Grandma has created for them. The sights and smells and sounds of their ancestor's lives surround their senses and make everything real. Within the helmet they can experience the details of how their ancestors lived. It all comes together to create new ideas and new avenues for exploring the past.

Groovy Grandma knows that virtually any aspect of history can relate to her ancestor's lives. These historical and cultural specifics are already in every family's life. She just connects the specifics to the people they came from. Any and all historical resources, such as books and movies or museums and classes, can help to fill out the details. Groovy Grandma lets her family smell and taste their past through the food they eat. They connect to their ancestors by trying the talents and skills that they had. Together they celebrate their family's traditions to enrich their own lives with a sense of tradition. They can almost hear their progenitors in the sounds of the music they listened to.

I only met my mother-in-law a few times before she passed away. The last time she came to visit, she taught me how to make the cranberry salad that her mom used to make. It has become a family staple and I'm so glad she gave us that taste of her life. Her childhood home was near acres and acres of cranberry marshes in Necedah, Wisconsin. Her mother didn't have a food processor, so she would do it this way:

Cranberry Salad.

Fill up the blender with cranberries and water and blend. Once the cranberries are ground up into chunks, dump them into a strainer to drain the water and then put them in a mixing bowl. The water makes it so the cranberries are easier to grind. Repeat the process with a whole apple, and then a whole orange with peel, and then a blender full of walnuts. All of these are ground into chunks and strained and then mixed together. Add sugar to taste, the cranberry salad is complete.

You can taste my grandmother-in-law's cooking when you try the recipe. Even though I never met her I feel like I know her. When you add some bratwursts and turn on the polka music, the effect is complete. I can teach my children about their hard working Midwestern roots and they can feel and taste and hear them as well.

Often the key to immersing your family in their family history is to be subtle. Are there any small tidbits of information surrounding your family's history that could create an "aha" moment? Most of the time they are already there in your family life—you just have to point them out and tell your family about where they came from. The culture of your family of origin can create a sense of identity for your descendants. When you teach your children about the customs of your family, it creates links of understanding that gives them a sense of their heritage.

We live in an incredibly mobile world. Many generations ago our ancestors rarely traveled or moved. Now we change jobs and homes several times in one generation. During the last few generations, these moves have created distance from our past. Most of us have left our family's homesteads and culture and thus the nuances of our family's history have been lost. We have lost track of the forces that shaped our ancestor's personalities and decisions. Consequently, we have lost an understanding of the forces that helped to shape who we are now.

Like Groovy Grandma, you can recreate many parts of your ancestor's world for your children and grandchildren. When you put the sights, smells and sounds of your family's culture in their heads, it gives them a firm foundation for learning about their history, and knowing their history can give them the knowledge and strength to make good decisions for the future.

Talents

Hopefully you know of some of your ancestors' talents. Have you ever stopped to consider that the aptitudes they had and excelled at are likely what you know most about them? Those talents and aptitudes have probably been exactly what has been talked about and handed down through stories through the generations. You are the next link in that chain. You need to repeat those stories about your ancestor's talents for the next generation. Your children and grandchildren can gain inspiration from the talented people in your family's past.

Talents are often associated with the arts. Performance talents might include playing a musical instrument, singing, acting or dancing. Other artistic talents might include painting, drawing, or sculpture. Perhaps your ancestor had talents in academics or linguistics, or maybe you have an ancestor who was good at speaking or making people feel comfortable, or being kind to strangers. Any of the good qualities you know about your ancestors is a talent that you will want to teach your children and grandchildren about.

When I was about 10 years old my paternal grandmother invited me to come stay with her for a week and she taught me how to sew. I learned to cut out a pattern and piece the fabric together and iron everything so that it looked right. I made a dress that week I stayed with her. I was so proud of myself and I enjoyed working with my grandmother and getting to know something about the skills she had. I've used that skill in many different situations, sewing clothes for myself as I became interested in fashion, working at a fabric store, and financing a study abroad trip with employment as a seamstress.

When I knew my grandmother, she was a retired Home Economics teacher and there was nothing domestic that she couldn't do perfectly. Eventually, she also taught me how to quilt. I inherited two of her sewing machines, and while I haven't made any spectacular quilts, I have made several simple quilts on my own quilting frames. I also inherited several of my grandmother's quilting books. Both my sons and daughter have enjoyed helping tie a couple of quilts and as we worked I got to tell them about their great grandmother.

There may be obvious or hidden talents in your family. My mother was a seamstress as well. I don't think sewing was something I was taught as much as something that already flowed in my blood. Is there something that has been passed down in your family in a similar way? Did you learn how to paint or write from your parents or grandparents? Figure out what they were known for and help your children come to appreciate that part of their heritage.

 Hit Them Where They Live Are there any talents that your children have that your ancestors shared? Was your great-grandfather into debate or sports? Did your great-grand-mother enjoy needlepoint? Show your child the pictures or heirlooms you have that are linked to their ancestors not only by family ties but also by the child's common interest. Once the child identifies with that ancestor because of the mutual interest, share other stories about that ancestor. Let them know that they have someone they can look up to with whom they also share a talent.

 Learn Something New That Is Old Maybe you don't know how to do something one of your ancestors did. Try some-thing new together. Explore a hobby with your child that your ancestor had or might have had given the time and place they lived. Take a class together or look for instructions at a hobby supply store. You can probably find instructions or videos online that will teach you how to recreate a hobby your family member had. Even if the talent didn't come down through the generations to you, you can still start now. You might discover an aptitude you didn't know you had.

 Heirloom Re-Creation Is there an heirloom that one of your ancestors created that you can create a companion to? Maybe you have a wood carving or some leather work or a handicraft from one of your ancestors. See if you can create something similar to the first, then teach someone in the next generation how do it. Now you have three artifacts coming from three generations of your family. You have just tripled the value of your heirloom. Future generations will have three family heirlooms to treasure.

Performances If the talent for performing arts runs in your family, why not try recreating a few performances? Put together a family talent show featuring several members of the family, or create a silent move together or a family play. You can use your family's history as a topic for the scripts or a theme for the show. Recreate a scene from your family's history in a skit or have a story telling competition. Be sure to record the event for future generations, and consider putting parts of the performance on You Tube so distant family members can join in the fun.

Skills

Your previous family members needed a lot of skills to get through their work week, and they probably were not the skills that you are using today. Most likely, you have ancestors who had to create their own food source with gardening, hunting, and cooking. You probably also have some ancestors who had to create their own surroundings through building, sewing and rug working skills. You may have ancestors who worked at machine repair or woodworking or blacksmithing. Most likely those skills are substantially different from what you do during your work week.

Many historic skills have largely been lost in modern life. You probably don't know how to pluck a chicken or trim fruit trees so that they will be more productive, but your ancestors wouldn't know how to log into their email either. We've traded some skills for others in this modern day. Exploring some of those past skills necessary to sustain life could help you learn a lot about your ancestors' lives.

My husband's great-grandfather was a skilled shoe repairman. We've inherited his shoe forms and the tools he used to create shoes. Unfortunately in our disposable world, my kids wouldn't even know that you could repair shoes except for this great-grandfather's story. To teach us more about the life their great-great-grandfather lived, my kids and I can research historical shoe repair and what each of the tools was used for. We can get to know him and his skills through these artifacts.

My grandfather was a fantastic gardener. He grew up on a farm and although he left rural life and lived most of his adult life in the suburbs, he always had a spectacular garden with lots of fresh produce for the family and the neighbors. Before we could do anything else, the first thing we did every time we visited my grandfather was to go out to admire the garden. Those fresh vegetables are probably what made my grandmother's cooking so good and probably why I like all kinds of vegetables today. Likewise my father knows how to grow a great garden, and he tried to teach me as a child, but I never learned to appreciate the weeding part of the equation. Consequently, my gardens aren't quite as spectacular, but I continue to try because I love the taste of fresh chard, plentiful zucchini and straight-from-the-vine tomatoes.

It is wise in this modern age to have a broad range of skills to draw on. Many of our ancestors stayed in the same line of work and even the same job for most if not all of their lives. In stark contrast, most people in the upcoming generations will change jobs and even careers several times during their lives. If they haven't already, your children and grandchildren will be learning skills to help them support their future families. As they also learn about their family history, it could help them explore some different skills that can diversify and enhance their abilities in the future.

Think about some of the jobs your ancestors had and what they might have done to support their families. Look around online and in your local public library to see if you can find any instructions on how to accomplish what they did. Bring your children and grandchildren into the quest to learn this new skill and spend some time together in the process.

Providing Food What skills would your ancestors have used to provide food for their families? Do you know how to pluck a chicken, trim fruit trees, or grow tomatoes? Did your ancestor have a farm? If you have room and the ability to do it, maybe you could grow a fruit tree, plant a garden or raise some farm animals such as a couple of chickens or a goat. Have your children and grandchildren help in caring for the plants and/or animals. Watch for insights into your ancestors' lives as you recreate some of their experiences for your descendants.

Creating A Home Explore the skills that were typical to women in historical times. Sewing, crocheting, tatting, macramé, rug working, lace making and etc. were generally learned by the women in our families to create a lovely home. If you know of a skill that one of your grandmothers had, give it a try. Perhaps you can teach a grandchild how to cross stitch or do needlework. You might have a fashion conscious teen who would like to learn to knit or crochet or make beautiful hats. Look for the right supplies and a good pattern at your fabric store or hobby store or online. Have the child help you pick out the project and supplies, then work on it together to create a beautiful expression of your relationship and your family history.

Typical Men's Work What skills did your grandfathers have? Perhaps they were builders or farmers. One of my grandfathers was very skilled at engine repair and had a whole garage full of every kind of imaginable tool. He worked on most every car my parents owned throughout my childhood even though he lived two states away. Teaching my children any kind of repair skills could come in handy in the future. Other families might go on traditional hunts together to stock up the freezer with deer or elk or salmon every year. What skills can you share with the next generation that might be interesting and fun for them to try?

 Do Some Research Find a book or online site about historical skills you are interested in. YouTube is a fantastic resource in this area because many people post instructional videos about skills they enjoy. Remember to start with your child's interests and see where they fit into your family history, but don't underestimate new interests that they might develop. Pick out a few skills and check in with your child to see which one they would like to try. Add some pictures and stories about how your ancestors relate to the new skill, and you have just made a new connection across the generations.

Music

Music makes the world go 'round, and it is also a great way to make your ancestor's world come to life. It can be an important part of the virtual recreation of your family's history. The songs they sang, the music they listened to, the instruments they played, and the music they danced to can help bring your family to life for your children and grandchildren.

Music is an incredible way to bring the past into the present. You may not be able to see what your ancestors saw or feel exactly what they felt, but you can hear what they heard. When you introduce the musical history of your family to your children and grandchildren, and teach them about the people who played that music, you bring their ancestors to life for them.

When my Grandma and Grandpa came to visit they always liked to take us on long drives. In the autumn they loved the colored leaves in the nearby canyons and we would spend a whole day out exploring, most often in their motor home. Grandpa would always have Big Band music playing on the tape or CD player. Glenn Miller, Duke Ellington, Count Basie and Benny Goodman hold wonderful memories for me, as I know they did for my grandfather. I could always imagine him and Grandma dancing to that music as they were dating. It would be fun to teach my children how to dance the Lindy Hop, the Foxtrot, and the Swing.

When one of my great-grandmothers died, I inherited her sheet music. I didn't know until after she passed that she was a wonderful organ player and that she often entertained her dinner guests and her family on the organ. I have learned to know her through the music she played. *Fascination, Allegheny Moon,* and *Vaya Con Dios,* among other songs, transport me back to her time in Southern California. In her collection there was even a song she had written and many of the pieces were labeled with her signature and her various addresses. I discovered that there were several songs she sang to my mother when she was child, and I have now taught those to my children.

It's time to face the music and bring some sound to your family history. It is good for children to have exposure to a wide range of music styles and most especially the music of their own heritage. You could negotiate a trade-off, listening to their music for a while in exchange for some time listening to your music. You'll end up understanding them better and they will understand their history better as well.

 Try Their Genre Play music from a time period or area where your family lived. What type of music did your ancestors listen to? Use pandora.com and create a channel using the genre with which your ancestors would have been familiar. Play some music while your children are doing other things and see if they ask you any questions about it. When traveling in a car you have a captive audience. Turn on some music and tell some stories about the people in your family who listened to that kind of music. Antique music brings history alive. For some turn of the century music try cadp.familychartmasters.com.

 Music They Knew Did you have any family members who played a musical instrument? Do you know what their favorite songs were? What songs did your grandmother or mother sing to you as a child? If there were any nursery rhymes or alphabet songs that have been passed down, make sure you continue them into the next generation. The religion your ancestors practiced is also a good source for music your ancestors most likely sang.

 Dancing Did you have an ancestor who was a dancer? My in-laws went dancing every weekend in the club houses of rural Wisconsin when they were young. Try teaching your children and grandchildren the dances you knew. Perhaps there are cultural dances that you were taught as a child. Teach your children the folk dances from your family's country of origin (you can find them on the internet) and help them identify with their ancestors.

Food

Food can be a great way to bring the past back to life. You can literally smell and taste what your ancestors experienced when you cook using the same recipes that they cooked with. When you cook for your children and grandchildren, make sure they know the history of your family's recipes; who made the dish in the past and some details about that person's life. And if there are any entertaining stories about how or when the food was used before, or who ate it, be sure to share those. Food is always a great incentive to spend time together. Use it to teach your family about their past.

Most likely the food you cook is already a mixture of the recipes that were handed down from your family members. Your comfort food is probably what your mother and father gave you as you were growing up, and their comfort food was most likely what the family made for them. Food has so many connotations and feelings attached to it. From celebrations to traditional ethnic foods to favorite foods, your cooking and eating patterns are probably already a demonstration of your family's background.

My ancestors were a big part of our family meals and celebrations. Mom eventually made sure that when we used a recipe she had received from one of her ancestors, we knew whose recipe it was. I come from a long line of good cooks. Apparently, being a good cook was a treasured skill in my family since some of the recipes that have been passed down have "Do not share this recipe, only for family members." written boldly across the top. I guess that means I can't share with you the recipe for honey candy that Mom makes for us during the holidays, and you probably wouldn't be able to reproduce my great-great-grandmother's egg cake anyway since it calls for a pinch of this and a bit of that. Just take my word for it. It is amazing, especially when toasted with butter and sugar on it.

I can share with you my great-great grandmothers' recipe for Cottage Cheese Hotcakes, though. It is one of our favorites.

Cottage Cheese Hotcakes

Beat 4 eggs in a mixing bowl. Add 1 pint cottage cheese and 1 cup sour cream and mix together. Sift one cup flour, 1/2 teaspoon baking powder and 1 teaspoon salt and add them to the mixture. When well stirred, fry 1/2 cup batter for each hotcake on an oiled frying pan. When the batter is added to the pan and the first side is cooking, fresh or frozen raspberries can be added before the hotcake is flipped. (This last part is my delicious addition.)

I hear that Cottage Cheese Hotcakes are an acquired taste although I've always loved the sweet and sour combination of the cottage cheese with maple syrup or raspberries. Luckily, I married a cheese fanatic from Wisconsin so he loves them, and the cheese gene was passed down to my kids so they love them too. It is an easy dinner meal when I don't have much time to cook.

Think about what recipes have been handed down through different lines in your family. Perhaps you have dishes or cooking utensils that your ancestors used. Old cookbooks are a great resource too. Look for the pages that were used the most. If there are special ingredients, you may need to find them at a specialty market or online. Present the food as a gift to your children, or better yet, make an event out of eating it together while you teach them about the background of the dish.

 Record Your Recipes You may just instinctively know some of your family's recipes if you make them often. When they are just in your head it is harder to pass them down to the next generation. Write down the ingredients and instructions in a way that anyone could prepare the food without knowing beforehand how to make it. Record the circumstances in which the recipes were used and who used them, along with a few details or stories about the creators' lives. Make sure your children and grandchildren have copies of the recipes. You can create a cookbook or just a collection of recipe cards. These collections make great gifts for any new brides in your family.

 Share Preparation More than just making the food for your family, make sure you include them in the preparation, especially if there is a tricky recipe where the instructions are complicated. Make an event out of making the food together. Some families get together to make complicated and labor intensive recipes like eggrolls, ravioli or tamales. Carefully display the pictures of your ancestors who made these foods but make sure they are out of any area where they could get damaged by a splash. Share memories of that person or listen to their music as you work.

 Involve All Parts Of The Family What foods were passed down from your mother and grandmothers? Don't forget Dad's side of the family, and be sure to include Dad's recipes if he was a cook too. See if you can collect foods from all sides of the family tree by contacting cousins and asking them for their family recipes. You may want to create a family cookbook to raise funds for a family organization or a family reunion. Make sure the kids get involved, too, by inviting them to submit their favorite recipes or by writing about their favorite food memory.

 Dishes Did you inherit any dishes from your ancestors that might be used in a family gathering? Maybe you have a special tea set that would make for a great tea party with your daughter and her friends or your granddaughters. My maternal grandmother had a set of party dishes that are beautiful glass plates with a little matching cup for punch. I received them after she died and even though I didn't have much use for them, I'm so glad I kept them. We used them for my sister's bridal shower and it was very meaningful to be able to symbolically have Grandma there with us for that special event. Most of the time when we have a party, everyone wants to use paper plates so we don't have to do dishes, but I love to do the dishes when we use my grandmother's party glassware.

Traditions

"Tradition, Tradition" sang Tevye in the musical *Fiddler on the Roof.* Even though the musical is about change and breaking with tradition, the character Tevye knows the strong pull tradition has in our lives. He proclaims, "Without our traditions, our lives would be as shaky as... as... as a fiddler on the roof!" Likewise you can bring some stability into your family's lives with some of the traditions that have been part of your family's history.

My ancestors live with us in the traditions we carry on during the holidays. We have several family traditions that I've grown up with that make the holidays special. We always gather on Christmas Eve for Minestrone soup and Clam Chowder, just like we used to when my grandparents were alive. We read the Christmas Story from the Bible then we go around the room and everyone tells what they have been most grateful for over the course of the last year. We end the evening with Swiss Bretzeli and English Trifle. My mom has always honored our ancestors with this traditional food. Our newest tradition has been to have a cooking competition on the night before Christmas Eve among my sisters and brothers-in-law with a secret ingredient for our dishes. That means we have created our own tradition to pass on to the next generation, along with some great new memories and a lot of fun together.

It would be hard to celebrate the holidays now without these traditions that ground me to my past and mark the time as it passes from one year to the next. On my first Christmas away from home during my college years, I was invited to Christmas dinner with some friends. They served English Trifle. It was like a love note from home, easing the pain of being away from family, and reminding me that I was still a part of them even though we couldn't be together. Christmas was OK because I still felt that connection through family traditions.

Traditions are like a love note from home that your children and grandchildren will take with them into their future. A tradition doesn't even have to be repeated very many times for a child to have fond memories and feel like the tradition is a constant. I've been surprised by how much my children value the traditions we have carried on, even though I don't feel like we've been consistent enough with them. When it is something everyone enjoys, a family tradition can create a lasting memory that will perpetuate into the future.

What traditions did your family have while you were growing up? If those are traditions that would still work for your family today, bring them back and celebrate them with your children and grandchildren. Again, don't forget all branches of the family. There may be fun traditions along your patriarchal or matriarchal lines or in the lines of the people who have married into your family. Some of our best new traditions have come from my in-laws and brothers-in-laws' families. As each new generation combines with other families, pick the best ideas and create a strong family culture that draws your children tightly into their heritage.

 Religious Or Ethnic Holidays If you know your family's religious background you can celebrate a religious holiday as an expression of your family's history even if you don't ascribe to that religious philosophy. Try some of the traditions that people of that faith participate in. Is your family part of an ethnic group with strong traditions? Take your children with you to a St. Patrick's Day parade or create a Cinco de Mayo celebration. Light the candles on a menorah for Hanukah and play dreidel with your children and grandchildren. If you celebrated some of these holidays as a youth, bring back some of your favorite traditions and share them with later generations.

 Holiday Traditions What specific activities did your family participate in when you were young? What traditionally happened on Valentine's Day or New Years Day? Did you have any May Day or April Fools traditions? Maybe Santa Claus left tracks across the floor or ate the cookies the kids left for him. What summer traditions did your family have? In our busy lives, we tend to spend less time celebrating the fun traditions of the past. Plan ahead. Gather your family together and teach them about what your parents and grandparents did on holidays. Honor your heritage with some of the food you used to eat and display some pictures or drop some hints about where these traditions came from.

 Family History Decorations Are there any holiday decorations that you could give a family history twist? Try decorating a Christmas tree with copies of your ancestor's pictures. Include other ornaments they might have used, or symbols of qualities your ancestors exhibited. Make a paper chain for Thanksgiving of all the ancestors you are thankful for and why you are thankful for them. Tuck family mementos into holiday wreaths or swags or create a family history display with your ancestor's holiday pictures. Start looking at your holiday decorations with a family history slant and see what you can do to explain your family history to your children in a new and different way.

 Antique Or Historical Decorations Have you inherited any antique or heirloom decorations? When I was a little girl, my grandmother told each of her grandchildren that we could pick a ornament off her Christmas tree. I picked a small fabric ball that she had hand-smocked in red and green threads. It has become a treasure in our household. We leave it displayed all year round. I remember the blown glass ornaments on my other grandparents' Christmas tree fondly because it brings back that childlike anticipation of the holiday and the visits we had from them. Unfortunately the originals were broken over the years, but I'm always on the lookout for antiques that remind me of them.

 Superstitions And Sayings Do you ever find yourself talking to your children and sounding just like your mother? What are the sayings that she used to say to you? "Don't stick your tongue out or it will get stuck that way." "Always wear clean underwear in case you are in an accident." Does your family have a few sayings, either quirky or profound, that you can pass down to your children and grandchildren? Are there little superstitions in your family that you could teach your children? Did your grandmother teach you to make a wish while blowing dandelion seeds, or eat your pizza backwards? Pass down your family's sayings and superstitions and tell them where they come from.

Another way you can teach your family about their family's background is by not particularly teaching them about their ancestors at all. Just teach them about the history surrounding your family in the time or place where they lived. When young people learn about the general history around their family's past, it gives them the foundation to understand more about their own ancestor's lives. Later, when they hear stories about their ancestors, they will have the context to understand what happened.

You can enhance the history lessons your family members receive in school. Look for opportunities to learn more about your family's time period and geographical location. Zone in on your child's interests if they exhibit a fascination for a specific part of history. Connect your family to your child's historical interest and you've made a connection that could tweak some curiosity about how his ancestors fit in to the past. Give your children and grandchildren the context of your family's history and they will be able to build on it later to really understand what their ancestor's lives were like.

When I was young, our local community had an annual Pioneer Day that we participated in. One year, we were in the parade and Mom made us pioneer costumes and decorated our red wagon as a covered wagon. I remember having several pioneer costumes growing up and using them for Halloween, for plays that we were in, etc. I think I became identified with my westward moving ancestors and was given context and a sense of identity from these activities. There was no doubt, even as a little girl, that I had ancestors who had settled the west.

My home is close to a living history pioneer village that works to recreate the experience of western pioneer life. My kids and I really enjoyed volunteering there for a couple of summers and learned a lot of fun little historical facts and got to know some great people. We are pretty good at hoop trundling, carding wool and walking on stilts. The kids loved the Mercantile and the old fashioned candy. Each time we arrived at the village it took about 1/2 hour or so for their minds to slow down and their imagination to kick back in, but it was so wonderful to be unplugged from daily life. It gave us time to enjoy the sunshine, read a book, talk to people and even learn needlepoint and weaving. Each of the houses we volunteered in had a different focus. We enjoyed talking to people and teaching others about how the pioneers lived.

Historical resources give children the tools to understand and visualize what their progenitor's lives were like. Many specifics in a certain time and place were common to all of the people who lived there. You can connect the dots for children while you are exploring these resources or connect the dots later, but learning about history in general will help the next generation as they learn more specifically about their family history.

 Living History There are all sorts of places and events that work to recreate history in modern times. Living history sites are like 3-D museums where you can try out activities your ancestors did and talk to people portraying historical characters. Living history is perfect for children because the interactive environment makes it seem like you've walked back in time. Look for reenactment events such as civil war battles or frontier men powwows. If your family lived in the American colonies or New England you might want to visit Williamsburg or Mystic Seaport Connecticut. Look online for other living history sites that pertain to your family's history. There are living history interpreters literally around the world portraying every time period and culture. Take your family for a visit and let them meet someone who can teach them more about the time and place where your family lived.

 Books About History My grandfather collected books about World War II because he served in the war. Those books help explain what happened to my grandparent's generation and the context of their quick courtship. While working on my British family history, I've become fascinated with Jane Austin because she lived in the same county and wrote about the same time that my ancestors were there. While I doubt that my ancestors took after Mr. Darcy, it has been fun to consider what similar forces might have affected their lives. For your children and grandchildren, look for books that are on the child's level and are written with an engaging tone. For younger children, look for picture books about the historical topic.

 Heritage Festivals And Founder's Days Are there any local festivals around that you could take your children or grandchildren to that might pertain to your family's history?

An ethnic celebration or Founder's Day festival in a place where your ancestors lived is ideal, but if you live far away, you might find a similar cultural event closer to where you are. At a heritage festival, you can find crafts and foods and entertainment that will teach your family members about their heritage. Perhaps there is a Greek Festival or African Arts Festival that will immerse your family in the culture of their ancestors.

 Culture Night Create a cultural event for your family to celebrate their family's heritage. You could focus on a holiday or time period such as a German Christmas or Japanese tea ceremony. Dress up for the occasion and provide simple appropriate costumes for the attendees. Don't forget to take pictures. Play music that pertains to the culture and make authentic food to eat. Choose some activities or play games that teach your family how you are related to the time and place you are celebrating.

 Museums, Historical Sites If you can't travel to a site with your own family history, see if you can visit a historical site that parallels the history of your family. One of the most fascinating historical sites near my home is an antique grist mill that shows all the ins and outs of how grain was milled into flour in an earlier era. The site doesn't have anything to do with my own family history, but I'm sure my ancestors came into contact with a similar mill so that they could have the flour they needed to eat. Your ancestors likely rode the railroads, so a railroad museum would give context. What other historical museums might teach you and your family members about your family's past?

 Movies, TV Are there any movies or TV series that portray the time period and culture of your ancestors? Have a movie night and watch something together. Make some food from the time period or place. You can point out similarities between the show and your ancestor's lives, or just keep quiet and enjoy the time together. Whenever your child or grandchild comes to understand that they have ancestry from a similar time or place, they will have the memory of that movie or television show to help them imagine what life might have been like.

 Language Or Culture Classes It is great if you live in a community that has cultural resources such as classes in the language or art or history of your family's past. You can check community centers or community colleges for classes pertaining to your culture of origin. Try your local library or the YMCA for classes, as well. Ask if you can bring children with you or if there is a children's or non-credit price. If you can find classes specifically for children you've scored big, but if not, make some requests and see if the program director will help you find other resources that your children and grandchildren will be interested in.

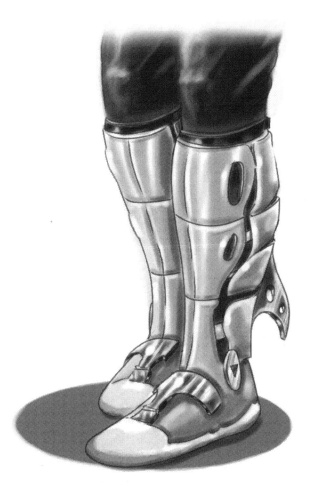

Section Six

Gutsy Grandma's
Super Styling Boots

Gutsy Grandma Pulls Her Posterity Close By Carefully Creating Today's History Together.

Life today runs at a frantic pace. Sometimes it is hard to take the time to associate with each other. How connected are you to the next generation in your family? Do you really relate to your relatives? It is especially important that older family members are connected to the newest members of your family. The older generation lends stability and structure—a sort of scaffolding--to the children in a family. It can really take guts to bridge the generation gap and get everyone talking and spending time together, but the rewards are worth it.

Gutsy Grandma to the rescue. She does her best to keep up with the grandchildren. They are busy, busy, busy. She keeps her little super heroes moving in the right direction with a comfy set of super boots. With these awesome shoes, they travel down the path of life together capturing all the fun life has to offer. Everyone feels buckled in tightly together as they spend time carefully creating today's history.

Gutsy Grandma has the guts to hold on tightly to her children and grandchildren. Together they keep in step with their extended family members, finding good friends and a support system that helps the children grow up strong and secure. They have a great time together organizing family reunions and family outings. They communicate and conduct interviews of older family members to learn about and preserve their heritage. They love to hear good stories about family members kicking up their heels, and they cooperate to make sure current histories are preserved. Family history celebrations are a party and even homework becomes fun when Gutsy Grandma is helping.

I found I have to walk the walk with my children and let them see me doing family history work if I hope to inspire the same actions in them. When I first talked them into doing a family indexing project when they were teenagers, I spent a lot of time teaching them how to do it, but then I got a bit sidetracked supporting them, helping them with questions, getting them treats, making sure everything was comfortable for them. It wasn't until I started really working on my own part of the project that they buckled down and got more work done. When we worked together as a family, pulling together at the same time, we gained a family unity and sense of pride in our accomplishments. I had to walk alongside them to really make that connection with them.

Likewise, one of the things that has worked really well with my kids is to "trade" them for family history. I'll play their video game or do something else they want me to do with them for an hour, in exchange for them letting me give them a little tour of their family history. It has worked remarkably well and I highly suggest you give it a try with your family. I have learned a lot about their interests, which has strengthened our relationship--a great thing in and of itself--but then they've been quite patient with me as I've plugged them in to some of the things they can learn about their history. There have been a few "hmmm" and "wow" moments that I know will only strengthen their sense of self and grounding in their roots. Every little piece of the puzzle helps put together that big picture that I want them to have as adults.

So, see if the family history shoe fits with your family. We've tried these ideas on for size and they have worked for us. When you set your descendants on the path of family history they will be moving in the right direction. Your whole family will really end up going places.

Connect With Living Relatives

An important part of giving your children a sense of family is to give them opportunities to spend time with their immediate and extended family members. When children know their living family members it gives them a feeling of identity and a sense of belonging to a greater whole. They can learn where they fit in the chain of your family and they will become the link that connects your family in the future.

A network of strong family relationships helps a child grow into a healthy adult. When a child is surrounded by the love of an extended family they will develop a healthy self image. There is a sense of belonging that comes to youth who spend time with their family members that protects them from looking for self worth in the wrong places. It helps when a teen knows his extended family well enough to actually lean on them for support if he struggles with his parent-- like all teens do at times. In fact, all strained and troubled family relationships are more bearable when there are other family members to lean on for help and perspective.

I was blessed to have all four grandparents alive until I was in my teens, and one great grandparent alive until my first child was born. We saw all of them often and consistently. I am so thankful my parents chose to live near my grandparents. We moved several times, living near both sets of grandparents until I started school, but even after we settled near my paternal grandparents through my growing up years we saw my maternal grandparents several times a year. To this day, it makes me happy to see the power lines in Southern California that look like "kitty cats" because that means we are getting close to my grandparent's old home in Los Angeles and it reminds me of all the fun we had together.

We consistently went to see other relatives, too. Mom and Dad worked to develop close relationships with their aunts and uncles. We also saw then when they came to visit my grandparents. I have fond memories of each of my grandparent's siblings, their cooking, their stories, their homes, and their families. I knew about how each of my grandparents grew up because I heard the stories from the mouths of their siblings. When I was very little, Mom faithfully visited her great aunt who lived in our city.

Although I was too little to listen much, and all I remember was that I couldn't touch anything, I knew who that person was when I learned more about her later in life. We often see my parent's siblings, too, and my children are growing up with a knowledge of where their grandparents came from as well. All of these relationships help me and my children understand the trends that run through our family and how they affect each of us now.

If circumstances don't allow frequent visits, you can connect with current family members over the internet through video calls. Set a recurring time for a group call to catch up with each other. Report on what has been happening in your home lately. Make an effort to stay in touch with your family now and it will pay off in the future when the next generation is surrounded by family members they know and love.

 Family Reunions Annual or semi-annual family reunions can facilitate lots of family history work, books, and presentations of family history information, as well as great story telling and some really good barbecued smoked salmon. (If you don't have a family member who travels to the Pacific Northwest to fish for salmon every year, you really should get one.) These can be fairly simple gatherings at a park, with a potluck picnic, some family history charts, and some tales about the great-grandparents. Your children will get to know your extended family as you spend time with them. Your family could arrange a vacation to a nearby lake or camping spot together, or somewhere else where you get to spend lots of time talking and getting to know each other. You can create a family reunion near the sites where your ancestors lived, or at schools or colleges that are able to host large events. Create identity with family reunion t-shirts or a flag with the family crest printed on it. Use some of the activities in this book to create unity and introduce the next generation to their family history while they are surrounded by their living family members.

 Letters I still remember my grandparent's address as well as my own, including the zip code, even though they haven't lived at that address for over 20 years. While my maternal grandparents lived several states away, my mother faithfully wrote letters to them every week and taught me to write letters to them, too. We loved receiving letters from Grandma and Grandpa and loved knowing that they treasured our letters. It was easy to write to my grandparents because I knew them and loved them so much. You can encourage your children and grandchildren to write good old fashioned letters to their family members with cards and pictures they've drawn. You can also encourage older children to send emails or texts. Write consistently, ask questions and tell the receiver what has happened to you recently—then throw in a little tidbit about some connection to your family history.

 Harsh Personalities Sometimes there are hard relationships that make relating to the relatives complicated. Truly toxic relationships need to be avoided, but if you have some family members that are merely difficult, you may be tempted to avoid them when introducing your younger family members around. Follow your heart, but be advised that some of the most important life lessons can come from adverse examples in your family. Uneven relationships can create knowledge that is just as valuable to a child as the happier relationships if you help the child process the situation. Perhaps you know where the trend came from or what circumstances led to the rocky relations. When you help your child see patterns in your family tree, the understanding you foster can excise that trait from developing family branches. Sample these relationships in smaller doses. Perhaps the unfavorable relationship should be held at a distance with emails, letters or Skype, but carefully giving a child the opportunity to learn from all branches of the family gives them that valuable perspective which will help them make good choices in their own lives.

 Visits There is nothing like just being together with the people you are related to. Take the children with you to visit their great-grandmas and grandpas, grandmas and grandpas, grandma's and grandpa's siblings, aunts and uncles, cousins, and every other family member you can find. Family history can be a good topic of conversation. Family members share common ancestors to talk about even if they share little else. Ask them what they know or teach them what you know about your family's past. Let the children in your family get to know other distant relatives their same age. And let them get to know the older members of your family. The more you visit family members, the more your descendants will come to know the breadth of your family's reach and realize where they fit in.

 One Child To Visit One of my fondest memories with my grandparents was the opportunity I had to go by myself to visit each set of grandparents for a week. My father's mother taught me to sew and introduced me to her friends. I got to observe my grandparents watching TV in the evenings in their study, while Grandpa read and Grandma did needlepoint. We went out for ice cream and Grandma had lots of time to tell me about her hopes for my future. When I was a little older I got to go by myself on an airplane to visit my mother's parents. I remember cooking for my grandparents, doing my grandmother's nails, and watching lots of the *Muppet Show* together. Can you spend a weekend or even a whole week with one child in your family? Pick some of the other projects in this book to do during that visit. The memories you make together will last a lifetime.

 Family Organizations You might want to organize some of your extended family members in a family organization to work together on common goals. An organization can be formal, with leadership positions and bank accounts and bylaws, or it can be informal with occasional meetings and shared projects. You can work together on family history projects and raise money for the organization by selling the family history items you produce. Or you might choose a service project and work together to help other families. Be sure to include the youth in your family and create opportunities to participate in the shared goals. And, of course, family organizations are the perfect place to get the cooperation needed to organize a fantastic family reunion.

Interviews

One of the best ways to help your children and grandchildren gain an appreciation for the stories in their family's history is to encourage the older family members to tell them. Conducting an oral history interview is the perfect way to get the older generation talking. When we interviewed my father-in-law he insisted he didn't have much to say, but 6 hours into the interview he was just getting to his high school graduation, so don't let anything or anyone dissuade you. Much of the valuable understanding I have gained about my husband's upbringing came from the interviews I did with my husband's mother and father. I learned copious amounts of information and I hope I endeared myself to them a little more in the process.

An interview can be recorded many different ways. You can record the voice in a sound recording or capture video of the interview so that you get both the sounds and images of the person during the interview. If you can't do the interview in person, you could even conduct it long distance using free internet video calling. Little nuances such as figures of speech, the sound of their voice, and laughter can be captured for future generations. Interviews give understanding about the person than you can't get any other way. You can use voice recognition software to transcribe interviews or you or one of your children could transcribe them using a word processing program. Make sure you let the interviewee go over transcripts and make any necessary changes before printing and distributing the final version.

Remember that voice and image recordings of the person you are interviewing will be very valuable in the future. Facts and dates can be researched by future generations but the personality, stories and mannerisms displayed in the interview are gone if not captured now. Make sure you have made good copies of the recording and share those copies with all of your family members. Transcriptions and printed copies are useful too. You can send your family parts of the interview as it is transcribed either through the mail, by email, or by posting it on blog posts. Put the interview into as many formats as you can so that it is more likely to survive and can be used in different ways in the future.

I remember as a little girl sitting and listening to my great-grandmother tell her life story on her patio as Mom recorded her history on an old tape recorder. I was enthralled with the stories about all her boyfriends and how they all wanted to marry her. (Perhaps my great-grandmother just knew how to tell a good story.) I got to hear about how she learned to drive a car even though she wasn't tall enough to reach the pedals, and how she came to meet and marry my great-grandfather. I learned about the hard work she did as a young woman, and how she managed as a single mother when my great-grandfather died at the age of 26. As I think about it now, I am amazed at how strong my memories of that interview still are 30 years later and how I came to identify myself at that very young age with my great-grandmother's fortitude and strength.

Check the internet for a list of questions to ask the person being interviewed. Search for "personal history questions," "oral histories" or "family history interviews" and collect the questions that will be relevant for the person with whom you are meeting. You may want to send the questions to the interviewee beforehand so they can be thinking about what they want to say. Make sure you include the most important questions, such as "What was the biggest turning point in your life," "What are you most proud of," "What do you regret" and "What message would you leave for your descendants." Along with the who, what, where, and when questions, the more thought provoking questions are really what will be lost to history if it isn't recorded now.

 Video While voice recordings are wonderful, if possible you should also capture the person's image as the interview is being conducted. With the family member's permission, segments of the interview could be posted to YouTube or another video sharing application for extended family members to view. Make sure the lighting is right and your sound equipment is good by doing a test run before the interview starts. When preserved and shared, the video will be treasured for generations to come because it captures so much of the personality and character of the person you are interviewing.

Transcripts My mother interviewed each of her living parents and grandparents and eventually these interviews were transcribed and published for us as gifts. Though they are only spiral bound, she embellished the books with pictures and other documents that illustrate my ancestor's stories. These books continue to be treasures in my life and I still go to them for strength and grounding. When I transcribed my mother-in-law's oral interview, I sent her sections of the transcript by email as I typed them and she edited them and sent them back to me. We enjoyed corresponding back and forth over this topic. It gave us something to talk about and I learned a lot more family information from her edits than had been contained in the original interview.

 Family Reporter Encourage your child to take the reporter's seat and do the questioning. Perhaps your child could interview several family members to create a collection of interviews. The interviews can be as short or as long as is necessary for the attention spans involved. This may be one of those times where rewards and bribery are appropriate if your child needs a little impetus. The payoff as the child gets captivated by the stories will be worth it.

 Tough Topics Every family has some family skeletons which may come up in a family interview. If you don't have a tough topic that some family members want to avoid, you just haven't looked long enough. How do you navigate the disturbing situations? Of course you will have to respect the mood of the interviewee. Distance of time or space will often help sooth family feelings and may prompt healing. In such an interview, focus on what the interviewee learned and what they want their descendants to take away from the situation. Those important insights are crucial because they help the next generations stop repeating destructive family traits. Treat sensitive information very carefully and consider the effect it may have on anyone still living, particularly victims. Some family situations may be better left alone until those involved are no longer alive. However, when descendants are able to identify and understand a past difficulty it often gives them the broad perspective that is such a valuable byproduct of family history. It may be that knowledge and understating about these hard topics is important information that descendants need to know in order for the family to move forward. They can move on with greater wisdom and make better decisions for the future when they understand the past. From deep pain can grow great joy when understanding ensues.

Send A Few Questions At A Time If you can't be in the same room for an interview you could send the interviewee a few questions at a time to write about and return to you in a letter or by email. Some people may want to edit their answers and go over them to make sure they are exactly the way they want them before they are recorded for posterity. This approach works especially well if there are hard subjects to tackle in your family's past.

 Interview Locations Take a tour of family history sites and let older family members tell stories in the places where they happened. You can give your interviews even more histori-cal and geographical context if you conduct them at an important family history site. Family members can describe what has changed at the site and how things were in the past. Being at the location where events hap-pened can often jog memories and help the interviewee tell the story with more detail and color.

 Photo And Heirloom Show And Tell Like taking the inter-viewee to a family history location, going through photos and heirlooms will help jog memories as well. Rather than recording the whole history of a person's life, you could just record a show and tell session. These stories can then be combined and edited into a larger history, or they can be left to stand alone as a collection of short stories about your family's history.

 What Was Life Like At Their Age One of the best questions my kids ever asked their grandparents was "What did you do with your time before TV?" We all laughed as we got a glimpse into how much the world has changed and how different life is now. It was very eye-opening for them. My kids got a real feel for what life used to be like and they understood their grandparents better in the process.

Record Current History

Your family can work together to create an ongoing, dynamic history of what is happening to the family right now. This might be done on a smaller nuclear family scale, or a larger extended family might participate together. Such a project could be a great lead in to a family reunion or might be an annual occurrence. As you work to communicate together about what is currently going on in your lives, you can draw together as a family, learn more about each other and capture your family's history as it is happening.

When family members live away from each other, it is good to know what is going on in each other's lives. Through the information and stories that your family members relate for this combined history, you will come to know them better, find more in common and ways to connect with each other. Even when you live close to each other and communicate often, putting together a combined family history may teach you new things about your family members. As you record your family history and find out what is most important to the other people in your family, it can be a bonding experience.

My parents have occasionally recorded our immediate family's history with a yearly family newsletter. As my sisters and I have grown and started our own families, we've worked to compile short family stories into a yearly family history. Each of us is asked to submit a page or two about what happened to our families over the year. While several of my sisters are great writers, the sister just younger than me takes the prize every year for the most creative history--including one last year that had lots of hilarious, wild made-up stories, along with the real happenings in her family.

Families who are living further apart could do this on a monthly or even weekly basis to keep all abreast of what is happening. This can be done electronically or by email and can be as long or as short as you want to make it. Make sure you have someone in charge of archiving the information for future generations and make sure it is sent to everyone in the family on a regular basis. Not only will you be learning more about your current family members but you will also be capturing the present so that future family members can learn about your lives as well.

 Yearly Summary, Monthly Summary Ask each participating person to send a brief yearly or monthly summary of what happened in their immediate family. The summary can be accompanied by pictures or video to include in the collection. You can suggest a specific theme for each summary or outline the desired length that you want. Giving a few guidelines for each entry will help the collection be more uniform and read more smoothly. Each contributor's personality will shine through their submission even within the instructions agreed upon by the group.

 One Manager Or Round Robin One person can be in charge of collecting all the histories and then sending them out to all of the family members, or it can be more of a group project with each person adding to the history and then passing it on to the next person. If you choose to create a history as a group project, make sure there are mechanisms in place for follow through in case the project gets stuck. As the history gets going and family members enjoy hearing about what the others are doing, you will begin to build a great legacy for coming generations.

 Collection Of Tweets, Facebook Or Blog Posts If you are social networking with your family as we discussed earlier, make sure you are collecting the family's communications into a history. Connecting to each other across the internet is good to pull the family together and strengthen relationships, but it can also create a family history while you are at it. Ask permission to copy information into another format for safekeeping or look for applications that help you collect the family's news. When you review it later, I would bet you will be surprised how comprehensive it is.

Travel

Family history travel not only gives you a chance to teach your family about their history but also gives you time to be together and strengthen current relationships. Traveling to a place where your ancestors lived is so much more than just a family vacation. It is a chance for you to share common ground—literally. The collective purpose of doing something together that defines who you are and where you have come from can really unify your modern family.

There is something tangible about being where your ancestors lived that engages even the most disinterested youth. Some call it a "spirit of place." Even if the landscape has changed drastically, the knowledge that you are connected back in time to a place and to the people who walked there is dramatic. Visiting a family history site fills that hunger and yearning to know our heritage with a real knowledge. Traveling to a family history site helps one reach across time and touch ancestors' lives in a magnetic way.

I remember as a 15 year old being very moved as I walked down the aisle of the church where my ancestors had worshipped in the 1800's in Neiderstoken, Switzerland. At that point I couldn't have told you much about them, and I wasn't very interested, but I remember the electric feeling of being in that church and looking at the walls that my family had looked at many generations ago. I learned a lot about their lives and the circumstances that shaped their choices by seeing where they had lived. It was cosmic to know that I was literally walking where they had walked. I'm so glad Mom and Dad knew enough about their immigrant ancestors to take us there and let me feel that connection.

One of my greatest regrets in family history is that I missed the weekend that my great aunt took the participants at our family reunion around to see where my great-great-grandparents had lived and where my grandpa and great-grandpa were born. I know where it is and I've been there, but I would have loved to have heard her stories. Conversely, one of my sweetest experiences with my dad was when I was able to take him on one of my business trips to El Cerrito, California, where he grew up. We were able to stop by the house he grew up in and visit the high school where he was student body president. We had a great time on that trip and I enjoyed listening to him talk about his teenage years. A trip to a family history site creates a connection like no other event can.

Is there somewhere close by or far away that you can take your family for a family history adventure? If time and money allow, make a complete vacation out of it, also giving each member of the family a chance to choose a nearby activity that interests them. Make sure to completely absorb the local culture, the food, the scenery, and the local people. Find out what life is like there now and you may find some insights into what life was like back when your family lived there.

Prepare Family Members For The Trip Search for the geographical history of the area and you'll be surprised what you can find on You Tube and on the internet to show your family what life was like. Combine it into some sort of presentation before you go, such as a Power Point presentation or Google Earth tour. Insert pictures and videos about the area and about your own family's history. Make sure family members know what their ancestors looked like and how you are related before you go.

Other Resources When you travel to a family site, look for other resources while you are there. Visit the local archives and check out museums and other local historical sites. Look for living history interpretations (people dressed up like historical characters) that might demonstrate what life was like when your ancestors lived there. Ask plenty of questions and see what the locals know about the history of the town and surrounding area.

Send Them For Research If you are able, go with or send your family member on a trip to gather family records. Long before I was interested in family history, my sister studied family history research in college. She worked with my grandmother on researching our family lines before any family history was available on the internet. (Remember: even though it seems like everything you need is on the internet now, there are still many, many records that are only available at local archives.) Because of her health she couldn't do it herself, but Grandma made it a priority to send my sister and my dad to Europe to research some of her family lines. They were able to make contact with several key archivists and extend some lines back several generations. If you have a child that is interested and able to handle hours spent in an archive, take them with you on a research trip. Two people can accomplish more than one. If the child is young, make sure you bring some activities for the time when the child is finished but you aren't quite done yet. Or, if the child is old enough, send them out on a research trip to find new resources about your family.

 Cemeteries Have you been to the cemetery lately to honor your ancestors and take flowers to their graves? If you live close to where your family members are buried, or even if it is a journey, you should take your children and grandchildren. I remember going to the family cemetery many, many times over the years, usually with flowers, often lilacs or iris from our garden. We would walk down the row and leave flowers on each family grave site and Mom would tell us who was who and how they were related. Make a treasure hunt of it, offering prizes for the person who can find someone you are looking for. Take a picnic and cleaning supplies to clean and make rubbings of the gravestones if the cemetery allows it. Memorial Day is a great time for such a trip.

 One-On-One Trips After I was married and had a family, Mom and I took a weekend trip to Wyoming to see where my ancestors had been trapped in an early winter snowstorm during their trek across the plains. It was a fun trip for just the two of us and we read through some of the accounts of the trek as we drove, which immersed us in the context once we arrived at our destination. We created our own family history event when we got stuck ourselves on a deserted dirt road and were luckily rescued by some passing hunters. We almost re-created our family history a little too literally and in so doing created some great memories together.

 "Who Do You Think You Are" Tour Take an older member of your family on a "Who Do You Think You Are" tour with members of the next generation in your family. Start where the person was born, and visit the places that this person grew up. Make sure you take a video camera to capture the memories that come flooding back as you visit the places and they describe what life was like. Visit schools, churches and other places around the home and let them explain what happened there. As mentioned earlier, being in the place can prompt more recollections than might come back otherwise. The younger genera-tion can catch the vision of what life was like by standing in the actual places where the events happened.

Events

If you are inspired and enthusiastic, you can put together a special family history event to help your children and grandchildren learn more about their past. This event can be an evening or a day or a weekend spent together focused on fun ways to appreciate their ancestors. Like any successful event, it needs to be geared to the attention span and interests of the children you are working to involve. Engaging the family with a festive family celebration can be the kick off for projects to come or reward for projects completed.

A special family event takes some planning and some work, but it is always worth it. Figure out who to invite and what the food and activities will involve. Choose a time when everyone can come. You may want to send out special invitations and make decorations that match the theme. Use some of the activities from previous chapters and plan some games to play together. Get into the party planning mode and give it a family history twist to make it a memorable experience for everyone. Involve family members by giving small (or large) assignments.

Every once in a while, Mom and Dad have gathered us for a family meeting with dinner and a story about someone that my mother had learned about. I specifically remember stories about ancestors who had crossed the plains as pioneers. When I was younger I don't know that I had much of an attention span or placed much importance on really remembering the stories they were telling me, but these stories have jelled as I've grown older and come together to give me a really deep understanding of who I come from.

Since we've become adults, my sisters and I have gathered once a month on Sunday evenings for dinner together—usually at Mom and Dad's house. These regular gatherings have helped our children become the best of friends and given us time to catch up with each other. We include those living far away with Skype or phone calls. At times a different sister has been assigned to tell a story or demonstrate something about our family history during these Sunday gatherings. We're working to make sure the next generation hears these stories even though they may not be listening any better than we did were when we were young.

A family history event can be a one-time extravaganza or a recurring casual get together. Don't rush things; make sure to reserve time for everyone to relax together. If you can, spread around the preparations so that everyone is vested in coming and the workload is less for you. This family function will help you strengthen family relationships while strengthening ties to their ancestors.

 Guess Who's Coming To Dinner Pick an ancestor that you know a lot about and plan a "Guess Who's Coming to Dinner" event. Cook the person's favorite foods or the foods of the region they came from. Display any pictures or heirlooms you might have from the person. Play music that the person liked or might have listened to, and involve a few activities that the ancestor enjoyed. Set a place at the table for that person and have everyone guess who the person is at that plate. After dinner, draw a winner from the guesses for a special prize and wrap up the evening with a Jeopardy style game with questions about the person's life.

 Scavenger Hunt Organize a scavenger hunt for more information about a person in your family's past or a branch of the family. Gather at a family history library or have family members bring their laptops for an internet hunt. Put together some questions about what you already know about that part of the family with clues on how to find the answers, then add a few questions you don't know and see if family members can help you find new information. Alternatively, you could post copies of important documents from a person's life in various places around your meeting place and make a list of questions that encourage players to read and understand the documents. Make candy bar prizes with specially printed family history wrappers that tell a fact or show a picture of your ancestor.

 Ancestor's Birthday To celebrate an ancestor's birthday, invite everyone to a birthday party. Instead of bringing gifts, have each family member bring an item that reminds them of that person and have them tell everyone why they chose that item. Have cake and ice cream and do something together that the ancestor liked to do. Make sure everyone leaves with party favors that have family history flair.

Toys the person would have played with when they were young, copies of family history documents or pictures make great souvenir gifts. Mementos from the party will continue to connect your family members with their ancestor.

 Family Show Put together a family show about your family history. Collect your family pictures in a slide show or Power Point presentation and have a competition for who looks most like whom, or who can identify the person in the picture on a family history chart. Google Earth family history tours make great family shows with embedded pictures and instructional You Tube videos, or watch your own family movies together starting with the oldest movies you have and moving to the most recent. Be sure to show when the children were born and ooh and ahh about how cute they were as toddlers. Make some good movie popcorn with too much butter and serve movie candy snacks to create the mood.

Support Other Learning Opportunities

There are lots of places in your child or grandchild's world where they naturally come into contact with their own family history. The history they study in school will at some point relate to your family's historical experience. As you point out where your family intersected with the events they learn about in school, your child will begin to connect the dots and gain a greater context for their family's place and their own place in the world

Family history encompasses all sorts of topics your children will learn about in other areas of their life. Your family is connected to geography, cultures, languages, music, art and literature in the time period and place where they lived. Any time you can observe what your child or grandchild is learning in school and say, "Hey, your ancestor did that," you have made a connection that the child will be able to build on later as they learn more about their family.

Though I don't remember any event in particular, Mom must have made comments about where our family was in relation to this or that history project at school. I remember knowing the family history connection when I worked on dioramas or reports about different parts of the world. Instinctively, I chose projects in countries and regions that I could identify with because I knew my family's past. As I worked on my assignments, our family history was put into context when it connected to what I was studying.

As I was growing up we heard lots of pioneer stories and I learned at a very early age that my family had been involved in the westward movement. Every time I'd see a pioneer story in the movies, on TV, at school or at the library, I knew they were talking about an experience similar to that of my ancestors. I became very identified with those hard working people and I took it personally if they were ever depicted in a less than heroic way. It gave me a context and a sense of identity when I saw my ancestor's stories in other places. There was no doubt, even as a little girl that I was tough and strong like they were.

When it came time to learn a language in school I chose German. In seventh grade I took a language survey class where we touched on French, German, Russian and Spanish. The class was designed to give us a taste of the languages we could then pursue in more depth. I remember feeling torn that French seemed very glamorous--especially to a seventh grade girl, but I ended up taking German. I just felt more at home with it. I'm sure my Swiss-German heritage helped that feeling and my knowledge of German has proven useful now when I'm working on researching more on my family's past.

Be especially helpful when it comes to school projects that connect your children to their past. You can help them study for tests or offer to edit school reports. Hopefully, you are supportive of your child's educational opportunities all the time, but in this area you can support them with your extra knowledge about the subject. Encourage participation in educational opportunities outside of school as well. Formal and informal academic opportunities will help your child learn more about the background and circumstances of your family's past.

 School Reports As your children progress through school they will likely have to do country reports and a state reports. They will also most likely do various projects related to different parts of history. If they have a choice of topics, see if you can arrange to have them research and report on places related to your family. Offer support to the teacher when you know something about a topic they are studying. Perhaps you can send appropriate treats or offer to make a presentation to the class. Most teachers love to have parents and grandparents share their own cultural heritage and you will be able to get to know your child's teacher and their friends better.

 Scouts Have the Boy Scouts in your family earned the genealogy merit badge? Ask your local family history center for resources that can help you with the requirements. It's a pretty easy badge to earn when you have the help of an interested family member. Your scout will be eager to have your assistance, and you can connect with him and teach him about his history in the process.

 Create Projects About Family History Many school projects can be tweaked to encompass your family history. Geography projects, dioramas, interviews and emigration units often relate to one branch of the family or another. Help your student recognize how your family is connected and illustrate the connections with any pictures or stories that you have. A child's school project may inspire more questions that you can then explore together.

Section Seven

Glorious Grandma's
Magnetic Magic Jewels

Glorious Grandma Works To Organize Her Family's Story So That She Doesn't Leave Brick Walls For The Next Generation

Do you sometimes find yourself overwhelmed with family history? Everywhere you look, there are more ancestors and more ancestors. There is always another line to follow. That's what makes it so fun, but you can accumulate a lot of information while you are following all those trails. How do you organize it? And more importantly, how do you organize it so that your children and grandchildren will be able to understand it and utilize the information?

Glorious Grandma knows how to find the jewels in her family history. She processes them and then leaves the family gems to her children. The stories of the past are crafted into beautiful pieces of heirloom jewelry. Grandma has a long term perspective about what is being passed down to future generations and how it is going to be presented. The next generations are captivated with the gleam and shine of the most important stories. They enjoy the lessons to learn from and the visual images of their family's past. Grandma's vast multitude of history information is smelted and refined. Her processing makes it easier to pick out the jewels and begin to appreciate the value of family history.

Glorious Grandma can condense her history into lists and books and charts so that it is accessible and ready to use. She carefully records where she has gathered the history so that when the children do more research they will be able to analyze and resolve differences easily to learn the truth about their past. Glorious Grandma is aware of the scope of what she is leaving so as not to leave brick walls of too much information that will overwhelm and crush future enthusiasm. She is careful to preserve artifacts in archival materials, preparing as best she can for whatever is coming in the future.

It must be remembered that your children will not only inherit your family's history but also the family history of the people whom they marry. Each generation doubles the amount of possible history that they may have access to. In this modern day and age, that means an avalanche of pictures and documents are becoming available because more and more historical items are being preserved. If you want your story to be heard, it will be important to have it condensed and told in an engaging narrative so that it will stand out as something of value.

In addition, in the United States we are a nation of immigrants. My ancestors are mainly from Switzerland and England while my husband's ancestors are mainly Czech and Swedish. My children then have roots in each of those countries. Each generation becomes more and more removed from the immigrant's experience and it becomes harder and harder to trace your roots. To gather their family's information, each generation must understand more cultures and countries as it becomes more removed from its ancestral homeland.

It is always best if you can pass family information on to the next generation gradually at special moments when the children can take the time to process it and value each jewel individually. This process comes naturally when you make family history a lifestyle. It is always such a tragedy when an older family member dies and the family either doesn't know or doesn't care about the precious family history treasures of the deceased. When family history information is sorted and organized it isn't as overwhelming to the people who inherit it. Start now to slowly teach and disseminate, organize and sort so that each jewel in your family history can be appreciated and treasured.

My great-great-great-grandparents left their home in Switzerland to immigrate to the United States. They settled near the Teton mountain range in Idaho where the mountains reminded them of the Swiss Alps. Theirs was a story of sacrifice and strength common to many immigrants. They formed a strong family bond and there was great love and family identity among their children. These tight knit family relationships reso-nated down through my matriarchal line. When their granddaughter (my great-grandmother) returned to Switzerland on vacation two generations later, she brought my grandmother a small, cloisonné Swiss watch to re-mind her of her beloved Swiss roots. I now wear that watch as a reminder of the strong roots I have and the loving grandmothers I was blessed with. It connects me to those ancestors and helps me remember to live up to their example. It seems all of their sacrifices for me are wrapped up in that watch as a symbol of their love for me. I reach a little harder to live up to my potential when I am wearing that watch.

Ideally, children will be interested in their family history long before they inherit the family jewels. Glorious Grandma has already been doing the activities and projects described in this book so that when the children receive photos, documents, or heirlooms they will already have a foun-dational knowledge and their interest is already energized. When they inherit family history that has already been organized, they will be eager to carefully carry it into the future and connect to the next generations in a magical way.

In the book of Proverbs Chapter 31, verse 28, it says "her children shall arise up and call her blessed." Surely that will be the case for Glori-ous Grandma when she processes her family history so that her children can access it easily. Then, it will be their turn to invest in the next genera-tion and make sure that each generation to follow is even more grounded in the family's history.

Scope

One of the most important things you can do to help family members appreciate their history in the long run is to manage the scope of your family's information for them. By its very nature, genealogy is expansive. Because every generation doubles the amount of information, and so does every marriage, before long you have thousands, if not millions of people to keep track of. It can be very overwhelming to someone who is just getting started and sometimes even to the more seasoned family historian. It is important to look to the future and consider the ways that your information will be passed down.

Have you ever thought that the family history information you are collecting might actually make it hard for future generations to find out about their ancestors? If you have collected a lot of genealogical research, you need to leave it to future generations in a format that is accessible and usable so that they can build on your information. You may have been able to break through research brick walls, but you might be leaving behind a brick wall of cluttered and unlabeled materials for the generations that follow.

I've inherited an abundance of family history. According to his journal, my patriarchal great-grandfather, Joseph Hatten Carpenter, wrote back and forth to England, collecting information on over 40,177 people. He worked to fit them together into his ancestral lines. He left 18 volumes of family history to my father's cousin. On the other side of my family, my matriarchal great-grandfather, Fred Schwendiman, collected information that was eventually passed down through my grandmother, mother and sister to me in the form of a PAF file with over 7,000 people in it. Likewise, other lines of my family's ancestry have been collected and researched with various levels of depth and breadth by various members of the family both past and present.

It's no wonder that although I grew up in a very family history oriented family, I really wasn't interested in getting involved with the family history records that had already been collected. Many relatives had collected historical materials but very little of it was in a simple, functional format. It seemed like they left me stuck between a rock and a hard place. I couldn't possibly gather and synthesize everything that had already been done, but if I started afresh, I would just be re-researching information that had already been collected. I was curious, but everyone told me that the first step in the research process was to collect what was already known about my family. That seemed impossible. I didn't have the typical brick wall of not being able to find information, but I had a brick wall of an overabundance of research to collect and break down before I could digest things for myself.

A major item to consider when you are compiling and organizing your family history artifacts and research is the scope of what will be interesting to your descendants. Organizing the amount of information and records that you pass down to your descendants is an art and not a science. You'll need to listen to your heart. Keep in mind that future descendants will have married into other lines of family history as well. When there is an overwhelming amount of information, future family members will have a hard time determining what is valuable to them and may be tempted not to engage with the history at all. It will be very helpful to your future family members if your items are well contained and well organized. When family history artifacts are left disorganized and strewn in boxes, they are harder to utilize. If you want your family's lines to be the ones that are remembered, make sure they are passed down to the next generations in a clean, clear format.

 Leaving A Brick Wall Of Too Much Information With my paternal great-grandfather's work, we were left with handwritten copies that needed to be digitized before much could be done with the information. With my maternal great-grandfather's work, my efforts to figure out what was in the 7,000 name computer file led my husband and I to start a genealogy chart printing service. I had to devise a series of charts to make sense of the information I had. The more information you leave to your descendants, the harder it will be for them to understand it. Consider leaving the most interesting parts of your family's history in a quick, understandable format with pointers as to where more information can be found.

 Weeding The Collection If something you have inherited is not valuable to you, it will not be valuable to them. Don't be afraid to discard or give unwanted items away to other interested family members so that the most precious parts of your family history can be treasured. eBay works great if the historical item might be valuable to someone else. Did I just really suggest that you would want to discard some of your family's history? Yes, I did. If your research is cluttered with information on friends and sidelines of your family tree, it will be too hard to determine what the most important parts of the story are. At a very minimum, consider giving away artifacts about your ancestor's siblings that might be more valuable to a cousin who is a direct descendant of that sibling.

 What Resources Will They Have? I wonder what Joseph Hatten Carpenter thought about the generations that would come next and if they would try to build on his work. I'm sure he could never have imagined the databases, the software, the iPads, and the Google searches that would be available to us today. I know he did the best he could to pass things down to us in an organized way. He searched for 20 years for the location of his grandfather's farm by writing back and forth to a foreign country. All I did was type it into Google Maps and within a couple of minutes I had the exact location. No matter what we do now, we can't imagine where the next generations are going to be able to take family history research. The resources that they will have, the tools they will use, and the ways they will be able to collaborate with each other are beyond what we can imagine today. Making sure that those intriguing family stories are at the forefront of your family history research will help them utilize the tools that they will have to find out more.

 Scan And Condense You can digitize and condense down your information into an easily accessible format. A three inch scrapbook can be scanned and reprinted into a ½ inch book. A bookshelf full of scrapbooks can be reprinted into one book that can then be copied again and again. Perhaps some of the less important parts can be left out. When you digitize and reprint, not only are you condensing the information, you are also disseminating the family's story so that each family member can have a copy.

 Process Into Something Usable As discussed earlier, one of the best things my mother did for my children was to boil everything down into children's books. These small digestible storybooks are infused with lots of pictures and memorable anecdotes. While the other extensive books Mom wrote are valuable for a more in-depth view of her ancestors, I'm so glad she took the time to write these smaller books too. Because I have both formats, we can dive in as deep or as shallow as the descendants' attention span allows.

Sources

One of the most important things you can do is to leave good pointers about where you found the information that you've collected. Keeping track of your sources is critical because sources give the future generations something to build on. Well documented sources establish the credibility of the researcher and the information. Future generations will be investigating the information you have collected. Well documented sources will help others in analyzing and building on your research.

I have a cousin who thinks Joseph Hatten Carpenter took a wrong turn in his ancestral research only a few generations back. If that is true, it is a landmine in his research, but it may just be that Joseph had sources that are unavailable to us now. For instance, a church may have burned down, destroying the records my grandfather had access to. Likewise, my cousin may have sources, through the abundance of records now available on the internet, that Joseph could not have dreamed of. Either way, the only way we can analyze the facts and try to figure out what happened is to compare the sources of their information.

If you have children and grandchildren who continue to trace their family history, it won't be a matter of if but only when they will come upon information that conflicts with what you have gathered. It is the nature of historical research that collecting different sources of information will sometimes turn up discrepancies. When your posterity runs into conflicting information and wants to look at the original documents you found, make sure you have given them some leads with which to start their research. If you are working with antique research, you may or may not be dealing with good references, but you can start now to identify them for the next generation.

Keeping good track of the sources you have used to assemble your family history information will help future generations but can also help you now. When you come into contact with distant cousins who are looking for the same ancestors that you are, they will likely have used other sources to determine what they know. You can collaborate better with people in your own research when you have kept track of where you found your information. Good source keeping can help to analyze what you find so that you can better ascertain what really happened in the past.

 Primary And Secondary Information When tracing your family lines, keep in mind the difference between primary and secondary information. Primary information is transmitted by the person it happened to at the time it happened. Secondary information is transmitted second hand by another person after time has elapsed. A single source can contain both types of information. For example, an obituary may have all of the death information correct (the writer was close to the information supplied) but the birth information in the obituary may be wrong (the writer may not have known the circumstances of the person's birth if it was long before their death.) Primary information should be interpreted to be more valuable than secondary information. Notations in your family's work about the origin of the information will be helpful to future generations when they analyze your sources against any new sources they might find.

 Originals And Derivative Sources Be aware of sources that are derivatives from another source of information. When family history information is copied, human error, bias, and problems with handwritten or electronic transmission may arise. Copies are the staples of family history research, but some copies are not as accurate as originals. Verbatim copies, corrected copies, summaries and selected portions can have errors in them. Likewise, published works and online databases often contain errors as well—especially when the sources of the information haven't been carefully tracked. It is crucial to your success in finding the truth that you drill down through derivative sources as much as you can to find original documents for your research. Trace the source citations that others leave to see if you can find the most original transmission of your family's history so you can avoid any errors that have crept into your family's story.

 Only What You've Seen It is important to only keep track of sources you have actually seen. If your cousin tells you about a birth certificate, your cousin is the source. If your great-grandmother said something that your aunt wrote about in her journal which was then cited in your cousin's book which your dad emailed you about, your dad's email is the only source you can cite, unless you go back and find your cousin's book, your aunt's journal or talk to your great-grandmother yourself. You should only record the actual sources you use, and remember, anything can be a source. When dealing with the micro-historical research of family history, your great-grandmother's memory can be a source just as much as the tea set engraved with a wedding date or a tombstone with death date.

 Direct, Indirect, Negative Family information can directly prove something happened in the past. Family information can also indirectly prove that something happened in the past. And some family history sources will prove something didn't happen—a negative proof. For example, two birth certificates showing your great-grandparents as parents may prove that your grandmother had a sister. A census record listing your grandmother and her sister may indirectly prove how far apart they are in age, but not tell you their exact age difference. A birth certificate for your grandmother's sister that is three months later than you had supposed your grandmother had been born will prove that your grandmother's birthday isn't when you had previously thought it was. Keeping in mind the differences between direct, indirect and negative sources will help you interpret your family's history correctly.

Citations

When you collect your family history information and organize it into a format to distribute to your descendants, you will want to make sure that any sources you have used are cited correctly in the final format. Whether it be in a printed work or a computer file, they'll need to know how you know what you know about your family. You may be tempted to just give them the whole filing cabinet with copies of what you've complied, but don't. Even if your family members want your filing cabinet of documents (which they will because as you've used this book you've taught them the value of their family's information), the filing cabinet can only reside at the house of one of your descendants. When you have correctly cited and compiled, all of your family members will be able to trace the sources of your information and then build on what you have collected.

I've taken several friends to the Family History Library in Salt Lake to look up old family group records submitted by aunts, uncles and or grandparents. In the little box their relatives were given to record the source of the information, there was often nothing listed, or a quick "family records" notation or something similar. My friends were left with little to nothing to work with.

In getting started with my own great-grandfather's research, my cursory glances through his information seemed to show that my great-grandfather was keeping good track of the sources he'd used. Glancing through his records, it looked like he had real notations on each page, and I had looked forward to building on his work. However, as we dug further into his research, we found that those notations, though blessedly consistent, were still very brief. Often they cite "parish records" for the places listed in the group sheets, but when we've gone to look for those records at the library, we've found that there may be several parishes in that vicinity. We are unsure which one Grandpa was referring to. It won't take much sleuthing, but it does leave another piece of the puzzle for us to figure out. I wish he had left a little more, but I'm so glad he left as much as he did.

When your family is ready to build on the family history information that you have collected what are they going to find? Are they going to be able to follow your citations to find the resources you were looking at so that they can compare it to current sources as they continue to search out more? The citations you leave are like the breadcrumbs that future generations use to find their way through your family's history. Is your breadcrumb trail going to be complete enough for them to follow?

 Complete Citations The more you can tell future family members about where you found your materials, the better. If your information is from a published resource, record the place where the document is housed (library, archive, home), the place in the document that you found the information (such as a page number), the publisher, the title and the author. If your information is from an internet resource, record the date the information was posted or accessed, record the location, and specify the publisher or organization that provided the information, the title, and the author.

 No Abbreviations There are lots of abbreviations of place names throughout my great-grandfather's work. I think there are two reasons for this. First, he was from England, and in the British notations we are working with, he felt that he didn't have to write it out. He knew what he was talking about. Sadly, three generations later, we aren't in England anymore and we don't know those places. We have to figure it out long distance, and that is tricky. Secondly, and in Grandpa's defense, the family group sheets that were the standard in his day didn't leave much room to spell out all the details in the place names. He did what he could with the space he had. We have more space to record information now and should rarely if ever use abbreviations in our family history records.

 Genealogy Standards To completely follow the current standards in genealogical source citation, be sure to consult Elizabeth Shown Mills' book, *Evidence Explained: Citing History Sources from Artifacts to Cyberspace* published by the Genealogical Publishing Company in Baltimore, 2009. Mills' book is a comprehensive resource for exact citations for every type of genealogy source. It is sometimes hard to accurately record the funny sources we find in family history research. Your information may come from the internet, a historical monument or the engraving on a bracelet. How do you write a footnote for that? This book will show you how. I also recommend her book *Evi-*

dence! Citation & Analysis for the Family Historian published by the Genealogical Publishing Company, Baltimore, 1997. In it you will learn about the differences between original and derivative documents, primary and secondary information and direct, indirect and negative evidence. Understanding these nuances can help you draw sound conclusions from your sources and also carefully guide future generations through the sources.

 Citations Don't Have To Be Perfect When you are recording the sources where you found your information, keep in mind that the citations don't have to be perfect. The number one rule is to try to record enough information so that another researcher can follow your path and doesn't have to redo your research. You never know what resources a future family member may have access to. If they come into conflict with some of your conclusions, you want to make sure they can retrace your steps and compare and analyze your sources against theirs to come to a new understanding of the facts. If you have done your best to represent the truth as you know it, show them where you found it so that they can continue to find the truth as well.

Analysis

While you are recording the source citations about where you found your information, it is a good idea to record any analysis you might have made about the information as well. Analysis can be one of the most important parts of source citation that we pass on to our descendants. You may know something about this source that would otherwise be lost to your descendants.

Was one of the owners of the family bible an aunt who wanted to hide an illegitimate birth? Or have you traced all the John Smiths that lived around your John Smith and you know which one he isn't? It is important to leave that information to your descendants so that they won't make poor conclusions if they don't know as much about your family as you do. Elizabeth Shown Mills wrote, "Once we refer researchers to a specific source, we are obligated to alert or caution them, as they may be less experienced with the materials."[1] Your descendants will not only be less experienced with the materials at first, they will also be further removed from the incident and they will need your analysis to correctly determine what happened.

My great-grandmother lied about her age most of her life. When she was quite young, the driver's license authority made a mistake on her license and recorded her birth year as several years later than it actually was. She turned that opportunity to her advantage, creating several more official documents throughout her life by using her driver's license as identification. She was a very dynamic lady and very worried about growing old. She even introduced herself as her daughter's sister in several situations. When I remember her best, in her 80s, she was very upset that her voice was starting to sound weak and people wouldn't take her seriously enough over the phone. I must leave a written record for my descendants of my knowledge that many documents in her life reflect an incorrect age and why, along with my knowledge of what a spunky lady she was. That way they won't be faked out by her little white lie.

---

1   Mills, Elizabeth Shown. "Citing Your Sources," *OnBoard* 1 (September 1995): 24.

If you know anything about the skills of the person who recorded your family's information, include that in your analysis. Perhaps you know about the purpose or reliability of the source's creator, or you may recognize important information in the penmanship or language. If so, pass that information along. You are closer to the family's history than future generations will be. Especially with the people that you knew but who have now passed on, it is important to pass on your knowledge of the whole situation. If you know more about the details or the context, make sure you record that information for your children and grandchildren.

As a family historian, you have the right to analyze the story and leave your version of what you think happened for your descendants. I tell my parents that if they don't write their own personal histories, then I get to tell my side of the story. That will be useful when describing my teenage years, don't you think? You can give your opinion of the painful issues in your past, the harsh personalities, and the family skeletons, but I would encourage you not to dig too deeply into other living family member's issues. Leave it to later family members to tell their own stories. Stay committed to the truth and document what you know so that future family members will be able to tell what happened.

 Unsuccessful Searches Leave a chronicle of the holes in your knowledge about your family. Have you tried to find out about a missing relative but not been successful? Have you found a brick wall when trying to trace a particular ancestor? Record your unsuccessful searches. Future generations will have resources we haven't even dreamed of yet. Their curiosity may lead to breakthroughs in items that were frustrating to you, but only if you leave them some clues and a clear view of what was missing.

 Preserve Evidence You Know Is Wrong If you find something that has been proven wrong with other sources, make sure to note it and why you know it is wrong. With my great-grandmother's life, my children and grandchildren will likely come across a document that suggests that she was younger than she really was. If I don't want them to be confused, I need to show them that I knew the document was wrong and why I knew that. You may have a published family history with a fact that you know is wrong. If you ignore that reference, future generations might think you didn't know about it. Record the information and explain why you know it is wrong.

Record What You Know About The Source You know more about the generations immediately before yours than future generations will. What do you know about the people who left you your family's story? What were their personalities like and how might that have impacted the way your family's information was transmitted. Do you have a relative that was extremely negative or overly optimistic? Record what you know about the reliability of the people who created your family narrative so that future generations will know not only the information, but a little about the people who created it.

 Differing Interpretations A member of my family who shall remain unnamed here was blessed with a particularly negative personality. The version of the family history that this person is bound to leave for the next generations will differ substantially from other's versions of the story. It is my duty to leave a more balanced side of the story that explains what happened. (My version of the story is right, of course.) Even if it is hard to determine the truth, future generations need both perspectives so that they can decide how the past unfolded. Don't be afraid to point out poor choices to help your children and grandchildren see the consequences of such choices. The perspective that family history brings will help future members of your family.

List and Instructions

One of the most engaging things about the family information you leave your children might be the lists and pointers explaining how the information is arranged and where they might want to search next. As you organize your information, make sure to leave instructions as to how you have arranged things. As much as it seems clear to you, each person's brain is a little different and they may not follow your reasoning. If you have organized your information chronologically, or by family line, or by the size, shape or format of pictures and documents, explain your system to them and it will be more understandable.

When you reduce your family history down to the best stories and the most useful points of information, see if you can also condense it enough that you can give it bullet points. No matter what the format, give the whole collection of information a table of contents or an outline as if it were a book format. You may want to list where heirlooms are stored and who they belonged to, instructions on where to go next with the research, charts of what you know about the family's relationships, and outlines of the most important stories and pictures. If you leave it in a clear and concise outline your children and grandchildren will be more likely to value and appreciate what you have collected.

My great-grandfather left us a few pointers to help us explore beyond what he did and be curious about what he couldn't find. In April 1959 he wrote: "I have now reached my 98th birthday and I feel I can do little more to add to my several lines of ancestry. I can do nothing more with Rev. Grubbs, Rector of Spaxton, Somerset, who has so grossly deceived me. I leave the further solution to my descendants to attend to it when Grubbs dies and a successor comes in who can more readily furnish the records of the Gibbs, Elliotts, and Carpenters of Tugswell Manor."[2] Thus we know where we can start to build on his research. In fact, one whole volume of his journal is about the genealogy he collected and his future plans for it.

---

2   Carpenter, George Alvin. *Highlights In The Life of Joseph Hatten Carpenter.* Provo, Utah: Self Published. Pg. 62.

Some days I think that all my children will inherit is my list of the things I still want to learn about my family. I have a long list of cousins who inherited documents and pictures that I need to contact, leads I want to research in the databases on the internet, places I want to visit and documents that need to be reviewed at different archives. No matter how much I learn about my family, there will always be more questions to be curious about and more searches to add to the list. Hopefully, as my children become adults, we'll divvy up that list and work on it together. Then, when I die, my children will be able to continue on.

It is such a tragedy when an avid family historian collects too much information and then leaves it in a format that is unapproachable or unmanageable for their children. Creating a system of organization with the waypoints and maps to be able to navigate it will help make sure that your information is valuable to the next generations. Remember that your children and grandchildren may not be as experienced as you are with your family history. Make it easy on them. Create lists and instructions that will help them know not only what you have but what to do with in. The added benefit to your organization is that it will help you be more effective now in your own work.

 What Still Needs To Be Done Create a list of people you need to contact for information about your common ancestors. Make a list of archives and libraries you would like to visit to find more documentation on your family's history. Create a bibliography of all the published resources you know which contain information on your family. Create a research planner with a list of resources you still want to explore. As you learn more, create a research log describing where you have looked and what you found. Keep these research planners and research logs organized so that future family members will be able to trace what you did.

 Color Coded Chart Print a pedigree chart color coded to the various lines of your family and then coordinate it with your family's information. Organize your documents into color coded file folders to match the chart, and keep photos and memorabilia in color coded scrapbooks. Keeping things organized this way makes it easier for your descendants to access the information, but it also keeps things organized for you, You will be able to find exactly what you are looking for when you need a picture to illustrate a story or a tradition you are sharing with your children and grandchildren.

Organization Hints No matter how you store your family's information, create a one page table of contents describing to your descendants how you organized what you have. If your information is in electronic files, create a readme document that goes with it and describes your filing system. If your information is in hard copies, create a descriptive document and place it in an obvious starting place. Of course, if your family's information is condensed into a book format, write a good introduction explaining how the book is organized and a clear, detailed table of contents. Integrate the information into a brief abstract so that your family can assimilate it.

 Shortcomings If there is something you weren't able to accomplish, tell your family up front. Is there a story in your family that is too raw in this generation but will be a strength to the next? Let your family know where you had to stop in recording your family history. Tell your descendants about your shortcomings as a family historian. Don't hesitate to give them something more to be curious about. Your stumbling block could be the next generation's stepping stone.

Archival Storage

While I don't recommend it, the best thing that could happen to your family's artifacts is to let them be forgotten in an archival box in a cool, dry place for a couple of generations. You want to use your family's treasures to teach your children and grandchildren about their history, but using them irresponsibly can be damaging to them. Don't lock your family's records up, but be very careful not to love them to death.

There are some things you can do at home to preserve and protect your history. The main rule is: don't do much. Many well-meaning people have done irreversible damage to their antiques, documents and pictures when they would have survived beautifully if just left alone. Be careful what you use to preserve them. It is your responsibility to make sure that your family's treasures make it into the next generation safely. When you utilize your family heirlooms to teach your family about their history, do it carefully, then make sure the items are safely archived.

My mother-in-law's historical items were assembled in various boxes and containers when she passed away. I was very blessed that the family entrusted these items to my husband and I. When we received them, we quickly went through and made sure that there were no destructive materials that would hurt the items in the collection. In the future, we will sort and process documents and photos and make sure they are disseminated throughout the family. Until then, they are housed in archival waterproof containers where we know that no damage is being done to them.

In addition, I was entrusted with my matriarchal grandmother's wedding dress. Years of storage in a humid climate had taken a toll on the dress before I ever received it. There were little brown spots all over the beautiful white dress. We took the dress to a special cleaner who deals with antiques. After the dress was cleaned and most of the spots removed, we carefully wrapped the dress in tissue paper taking care not to create any creases. We then stored it in an archival box in my closet so that it is available when my grandchildren want to learn more about their great-great-grandmother.

When you are entrusted with a family heirloom, you have received a general obligation to future generations. If you take good care of the artifact, they will be able to share an item that will be older and even more rare and more precious than the one you received. If you are the one who ruins that item, you will create an unnecessary road block to their understanding of their past. You should carefully archive any family history treasures you have been entrusted with so that future generations can appreciate your common heritage.

 Use Archival Materials All of the products mentioned in this chapter are available at University Products (www.university products.com), Hollinger Corp (www.hollinger-corp.com), Light Impressions (lightimpressionsdirect.com) and Gaylord Library Supply Company (www.gaylord.com). You can call and ask for a catalog from any of these companies. Their catalogs give good information about the latest archival techniques. These companies have all the materials you need to be able to protect your family's historical artifacts.

 Remove Anything Destructive There are a few things you should do with all photographs or documents you have. First, remove any staples, paperclips, rubber bands, string or anything else that can create creases or rust lines. It is also important to take uneven pressure off each item so that there aren't any pressure points creating creases or folds. Never apply archival tape to the photo side of a picture or regular tape to any part of a picture or document, and never apply any kind of tape to negatives or transparencies. And, of course, never fold or roll any important pictures or documents. Folds will damage the chemicals on a photo, and rolled pictures will be damaged when someone unrolls the picture to look at it.

 Don't Touch Too Much The very first thing to do before you deal with original photographs or documents is wash your hands and put on some white cotton gloves. By far the most damaging thing you can do to your artifacts is love them to death. Besides fingerprints, the oils on your fingers can do lots of damage, even when you are careful. A soft brush is helpful to remove dust and loose dirt if the collection has been sitting for a while. Temporarily slide items into polypropylene sleeves to reduce contact while you organize and identify everything.

Set Aside A Work Area When you are working to archive a collection of artifacts, it is best to set up a work space where you can leave things out until your project is completed. First, go through the collection to get an idea of how you want to organize the information and who and what time periods are represented. Make sure you have good lighting. Make digital copies so that you can then preserve and put away the originals.

 Preserve The Order If you are lucky enough to inherit a collection of pictures and/or documents, be sure to preserve the order of the collection as you initially go through it. Clues about unlabeled pictures—such as where the pictures came from and in what order they were accumulated--may be deduced by the other items around them. An easy way to preserve the order is to take several digital photographs as you initially unpack the collection. That way you will have a digital record to consult when you need clues about the items. Separate out the items that need to be taken to relatives for identification and anything that may need to be taken to a professional archivist, then you can start labeling, boxing and indexing each piece.

 Reversals From the very beginning, make sure that any treatment you do is completely reversible. You never know what advancements will be made in archiving practices and you should do everything you can to ensure that your artifacts will be available for future advancements. In 100 years, the document that you are holding which isn't very old now could be one of the oldest documents your future family member has and a very important part of their family history. Make sure that you aren't the one who damages it. Make sure that nothing you add to it is permanent.

 Donations In some cases, you might consider donating your collection to an archive. Archives usually provide a safer home and will make the items available to a larger audience. An archivist typically wants to see a collection before it is organized but you can usually help identify items as they are archived. You should be aware that most archives will want you to transfer ownership and copyright privileges before they invest the money and labor in archiving your collection. If you do decide to donate your collection, make sure the contract states what you want them to do with any discards. Be sure to get an appraisal for tax deduction purposes. If possible, it's a good idea to supplement your donated collection with a monetary donation to take care of the collection. Whether you donate the originals to an archive or not, be sure to share electronic and paper copies with websites and your family so that many copies will survive into the future.

Archiving Photographic Materials

The visual history of your ancestors is, in my opinion, the most important part of your family history because it is the part that breathes life into stories and vital statistics. Photos are the most important artifacts you can preserve if you want to involve the next generation in your family history. While researching your family's history, you may have come across a few pictures or a lot, but no matter what you have accumulated, you definitely want to make sure they last for coming generations.

Your photographic images should be protected from temperature fluctuation, humidity, light, handling, insects, dust and the gasses from other acidic storage materials. The best way to protect them from most of these problems is to keep them in the living area of your house. The temperature that is most comfortable for you is also the best for your images and documents.

Make digital copies of the most important photographs so that you can archive the originals. Use the copy to tell the story of your family through scrapbooks, charts, and other displays of the image, while the original is safely put away for future generations to enjoy. You can scan or take a high quality digital camera picture of the image to create an electronic copy, but try to keep the copying to a minimum because of the light danger involved. If you have a good copy you can put the original away in a safe place where it will be protected from too much handling. Loving a picture is usually the most damaging thing that can happen to it.

All of my mother's family history and childhood photos come down to us in painstakingly created scrapbooks that my maternal grandmother put together. After she was diagnosed with Multiple Sclerosis, my grandmother was confined to a wheelchair with limited use of her arms and legs, but she didn't let that stop her from doing one thing that was really important to her. She painstakingly put all of the family pictures into scrapbooks and labeled each of the pictures. As her disease progressed and took much of her mobility, she worked for long hours pecking at the typewriter with just a finger or two to create the notations for each of the pictures. Towards the end of the project, someone (sometimes me) needed to help her place the pictures and the notations slips, but she completed 6 scrapbooks that have all of hers and my grandfather's lives and the childrens' early lives organized and recorded.

My grandmother's scrapbooks were created with what were considered the best system at the time. Unfortunately the materials were not archival. As the pictures have faded and the materials have made it hard to save the actual photographs, we are still grateful that Grandma recorded the dates and people involved in the pictures. At least we've been able to scan the pictures and preserve them that way. We wouldn't have been able to do much with them had they been left scattered in different places, unorganized and undocumented.

Even though you will want to store some of your most precious family history photos where they will be safe, make sure they are still accessible to your family. Visual representations, especially photographs, powerfully connect your family with their family history. Display copies throughout your home so the family you live with—as well as family members who visit—will come to know what their ancestors looked like. Share photos online through social networking. Classic photos that are archived and stored should be copied and out on display in as many creative formats as possible.

 Types Of Antiques An important part of understanding archival techniques for photos is to understand how they are made. All photos consist of 1) an emulsion layer, 2) a base, and 3) an adhesive. The emulsion layer consists of the chemicals that make the lights and darks show up in the picture. The base is whatever holds the emulsion together. The adhesive is another chemical compound that lies in between the emulsion and the base, holding the emulsion to the base. As the craft of photography developed, photographers experimented with many kinds of base materials. If you have a daguerreotype, ambrotype or tin type you have a real treasure. Be very careful with these photographs because the emulsion layer is extremely sensitive.

 Strengthen The Base Currently, the best restoration I would recommend for an antique photo is to use a little Filmoplast to mend the back of a photo on a paper base. Filmoplast is a very thin tape with a light adhesive that is removable. Never use anything like Filmoplast on the front of the photo or it will lift the emulsion layer. Make sure the picture is resting on a stable background so that there won't be added stress on the image. You can strengthen the base of a picture but there isn't really anything you can do to the emulsion layer.

 Common Versus Precious When storing your photographs, you will want to decide which photographs and documents are the most important to you and store them differently than the rest of your collection. You may want to spend a little money to make sure that your great-grandmother's wedding picture is well taken care of, but the 34th picture of you and your dog or cat may not be important enough to warrant such expensive treatment. More common pictures can be mounted with photo corners on archival paper and then inserted into acid-free polypropylene sleeves and kept in a scrapbook binder. Don't forget to label the pictures on the archival paper and write about the stories surrounding the picture.

For your most important photographs, once they are copied you can lay them flat, interleaved with un-buffered tissue paper in short archival photo boxes matched to the size of the picture. Keep like-sized photos in the same box. Have several different sized boxes so that a smaller photo doesn't leave uneven pressure marks on a larger photo it has been stored under. Label the outside of the boxes to keep handling to a minimum when you are looking for a certain picture. Keep daguerreotypes, ambrotypes and tintypes in their own separate boxes. Archival four-flap envelopes are also good for protecting each photo from others around it and the envelope gives you lots of space for labeling while protecting the picture from uneven pressure.

 Antique Scrapbooks If you have an antique scrapbook you want to preserve, it can be hard to decide how to take care of it. A scrapbook can be an archival item in and of itself. A friend of mine inherited two scrapbooks from her great-grandfather. The first was a series of Carte de Visite tucked into cuts made in black acidic paper—postcards that he had sent home from a trip to Europe at the turn of the century. The second was a scrapbook he had made for his oldest child as a gift for the baby's first Christmas. The pictures in the first scrapbook were easily removed and had writing on the back that she wanted to be able to see, so she took that scrapbook apart. The second scrapbook was glued together and a sweet memoir of the grandfather's love for his new son in his personal handwriting. She decided to leave the second intact. You can interleave the pages of an intact scrapbook with tissue paper to help protect the pages from each other, so long as the additional tissue paper doesn't stress the binding. Storing the scrapbook in an archival box will also help it last longer.

 Protection From Acidic Materials If you have scrapbooks that you want to take apart, getting the pictures out can sometimes be a challenge. The magnetic scrapbooks with stripes of glue that were popular in the 60s and 70s can be especially challenging. My grandmother's pictures are in such scrapbooks. While we have been unsuccessful in getting the pictures out, other people have had success using non-waxed dental floss, heating the glue with a blow dryer, and using an X-Acto knife. In our situation, we have had to scan and copy and get them out of that format, as the glue is creating stripes in the actual pictures. Scanners and digital cameras are your best bet when a picture is deteriorating and you can't do anything to change the situation.

 Protect Negatives Another important part of archiving photographs is to protect the negatives. When you have good negatives, you can actually send two copies of the picture into the future giving them a higher chance of survival. You can also store negatives in polypropylene or polyester sleeves, or if they are more important, in archival four flap envelopes in an archival box. Several years ago when my washing machine flooded our house, water rained down on the bottom floor right on top of my family history negatives. When I opened the soaked archival box, I was thrilled to find the negatives and four flap enclosures completely dry. Needless to say, I was more than happy to spend $30 on another good archival box. Had they been in a regular shoe box they would have been destroyed.

Archiving Document Materials

Archiving family documents is a very similar procedure to the one outlined previously for photographs. Most documents can be archived on acid free, lignin free paper with photo corners and stored in albums in polypropylene or polyester (mylar) sleeves. This makes for a great way to organize actual documents with other copies and notations that you have accumulated. As with all family history, be sure to keep good notations about where you found your information.

You can organize your documents into albums or keep them in a filing system. On the paper the document is mounted to, or on the outside of the file folder, record a complete citation for what the document is and where you found it. Make a notation on which family member it relates to and what it tells you about the family member. Record any analysis or interpretation so that future family members will be able to interpret the document correctly.

After my husband and I were married, I created a wedding album containing the important documents relating to our courtship and marriage. I included letters and cards we had sent each other, flyers for events and tickets for special dates. Of course our wedding announcements and journal entries were included along with the marriage certificate. I wrote a lot of commentary telling the story of our courtship and subsequent wedding. All of it is organized in a format that is accessible to my children and grandchildren so that they can learn about what our lives were like before they were born.

When you keep your family history documents safe and organized you are providing your descendants proof of the past. You are giving them the stepping stones to use in the future when they want to find out more about their family. Rather than having to organize what you've done before they can go forward, they will be able to start their research where yours left off. Keeping the documents of your family's history safe gives your children and grandchildren the gift of a wide open research path.

Common Versus Precious Similar to photographs, while every family history document is precious, some documents may be more important than others. Original documents, and documents showing your ancestors' handwriting need to be more carefully preserved than copies and replicas. With your most precious treasures, you will want to spend more on archival materials to make sure that the document is preserved well into the future. The better you can take care of a document, the more likely your grandchildren many generations later will one day handle it.

 Encapsulation Very important or odd-sized documents can be encapsulated for greater safety. Encapsulation is sealing a document between two sheets of polypropylene. An archival double sided tape is placed around the outside edge of the sheet and the document is placed carefully inside the tape. A second sheet of polypropylene is then secured on top of the document and sealed with the tape. The document floats freely inside the two sheets and the process is fully reversible since no adhesive is touching the document. When done correctly, encapsulation forms a vacuum seal against air and other contaminates that might cause the document to deteriorate, and the person viewing the document will be able to see both sides of the record.

 Keep Reversible Laminating a document for preservation is one of the worst things you can do. Most lamination will turn brittle and yellow over time, and more importantly lamination is irreversible. You never know what someone might be able to do to better preserve the document in the future. Unlike encapsulation, laminating destroys the document when you try to remove it.

 Copying When you are ready to make copies to display or disseminate, print with the right kind of ink and paper. If not, your new copy may go bad faster than the original. Look for printers that use pigment inks, DuraBrite inks and Ultrachrome inks and papers. In this area, you usually get what you pay for. Inexpensive inks and printers are usually not archival.

Archiving Digital Materials

When it comes to digital restoration and archiving, the most important thing to remember is that scanning something into the computer is not necessarily archiving it. You must take care of digital copies even more diligently than hard copies. When you have digitized something you have made it easier to share, easier to disseminate, easier to copy, easier to restore and easier to index. However, when you create an electronic copy of something you have not preserved it. Computers die and are replaced. Technology changes. Files are easily lost and forgotten. Digital copies of photographs are good to have for repairing the image, or sharing and copying, but technically, your paper copies are very likely to survive longer into the future than any digital copies.

When deciding how to preserve your information for the next generation you need to think about how your family will best access the information and in what format it will most likely be used. Often the best thing you can do is print copies because prints are less likely to get lost or deteriorate than digital copies. Paper copies or books are also more likely to be read and used if they are tangible and available. However, as our lives become digitized and mobile, more of our focus moves to the computerized world. There are more avenues popping up every day for storing and using information in new ways, including ones we may not have thought of yet. Certainly, attracting the next generation should include digital images and stories where they are most likely to access them. As they get involved, they will find new ways to be creative with their digitized history.

Unfortunately, when you digitize something you have put it at higher risk for disappearance. Digital materials can be much more fragile than physical materials. There are four main threats to digital data. (1) In the future, your digital family history may be hard to retrieve and buried with useless information. (2) It may have physically deteriorated. (3) It may electronically lapse or be purposely destroyed, or (4) it may be in an unusable format and digitally obsolete. In some ways we are risking a digital dark age with the current digital records we are creating. Future generations may actually know more about the generations before us than they do about us because our digital records may have deteriorated when the physical records of our ancestors may still be available. For example, my grandparents communicated through letters, my parents communicated over the phone, my husband and I communicate through emails, and my children will communicate with their future spouses through texts and other ways not yet invented. My grandparent's letters may be the only things left for my grandchildren to read to get to know any of us who are gone.

If you had to produce an important email you sent 12 years ago could you do it? Probably not. I recorded and digitized my mother-in-law's oral history many years ago. We made recordings and I transcribed it to Word Perfect version 7 on a computer running Windows 95. This personal history became priceless to my family when she died only a couple of years later. My children don't remember their grandmother because they were only toddlers when she passed away. The major record we have of her life, revealing her personality, her character and her family of origin is in this important document. However, in spite of how crucial this document is to my children's understanding of one fourth of their lineage, the digital copy has been lost. Somehow it did not migrate onto new machines and into the newest formats. Luckily, we printed it and gave copies to all of our family members. With a precious hard copy, my children will now have several avenues through which they can manage this information in the future.

To avoid a Digital Dark Age in this generation, we must ensure that our digital records are accessible and useable for the future. The way we manage the records we create has to keep pace with digital record creation. You can make a difference in your family by doing your best to preserve your own documents. With attention and a plan, you can preserve your records and not become the Digital Dark Age generation.

 Migration Plan Many problems with lost computer data can be solved by making sure the digital information you have is always migrated on to the newest computer system. Keep an updated, printed list and guide to all the genealogical files on your computer(s). When you buy a new computer, take the time necessary to transfer all of your files. When you purchase new computer software, take the initiative to make sure that all of your files are transferred and updated in the new file format. Migration issues are solved by budgeting time and money. When digital data is allowed to sit on a computer that is getting out of date, even though the computer is functional, if too much time elapses before the data is moved to a new computer, some of the files may be hard to transfer. When the time and money are allocated on a regular schedule to migrate to the newest systems, data will be kept viable for the next generation. If possible, make saving for technological advancements part of your regular family budget even if the budget is small.

 Naming, Tagging And Filing Being able to find the file may be as important in the future as making sure the file survives. As anyone who has had a digital camera for very long knows, it can be hard to keep files organized so that a certain picture can be found. The same holds true for family history files. Being able to find the information you are looking for may be tricky if it is lost in a lot of other data. Always name files and keep a current, consistent filing system so that items can be sorted and searched. You can also tag files in the metadata of a file so that searching is easier later. Computer filing and naming systems are like any filing system. It takes time to keep a house or office clean and organized the same way it takes time to keep your digital files organized.

 Refreshing And Backing Up To preserve your digital data and make sure it is accessible to future generations, you will want to have a plan for backing up your data so that you don't lose it before it even gets to them. Hardware failure is incredibly common and yet we often don't take the time to make sure we have created sufficient copies to insure against loss. Travel drives and external drives are great for backing up and can be a long term solution, but, they are as susceptible to failure as any other piece of computer hardware. They are only as effective as the person who is using them. If you forget to back things up for a while, you may find yourself missing your recent work.

Online backup services or the cloud (storing information on the internet) can be very effective, especially in the case of a fire or office loss. Being offsite, these services can be a protection against local disasters. You can store your data anywhere that will accept your files and keep them in a format where you can retrieve them. Services such as Carbonite or Backblaze can be configured to back up your data automatically. Other services such as Dropbox or an offsite server give you access to your data from different locations. All of these services require a password for data access and will be unavailable to anyone who doesn't have the password. They can be a life saver when you are dealing with data loss. Back-up systems need to be redundant and easy. It is best to not to rely on only one backup system, and make sure that at least one of your systems does not rely on you to remember to do it.

 Replication In Different Formats When you think about future generations accessing your data and pictures, do you think they will be able to find computer programs that will be able to read that data? Most software programs change quickly with new versions coming out every year or two. Only a decade ago, we were using different programs for word processing and images. Current software cannot read all file types that were used 10 years ago, but they have usually been written to read at least the most common types of files used back then. In order to make sure your files are readable, you will want to make copies in the most common digital formats: images in .jpg or .tiff, documents in .txt or .rtf, genealogy and databases in .ged or .csv, and document images in .pdf. Future programmers will make sure their programs read those files. They will be in demand since they are the most commonly used file formats now. In addition, saving data in more than one format will ensure that there is a file that will be useable in the future. At least one of the files should be readable.

 Data Recovery If you do experience a data loss, rest assured there are some rescue measures that may be able to help you. If it is a hardware failure, be careful not to write over the lost files and get the hardware to a data recovery professional as soon as possible. Recovery professionals may cost a lot, but they can be lifesavers if you are unable to reclaim your information any other way. If you are struggling with a file that is unreadable in a current system format, many archives try to support emulation—reestablishing old programs and computer systems. Some Family History Centers have a computer in the back room with old versions of software and old hardware such as floppy disk drives. Making sure you have multiple copies in different formats in several locations can ensure that you never need to rely on such a recovery system.

 Digital Will You may have put a lot of your family history information on the internet for your family members to access and enjoy. Are you thinking about the long term storage of that data? If you participate in an online family history database, your information may not be available to your family in the future. Online genealogy sites are great for finding new information and making sure your research is available to current family members, but when you share your information online, you either (1) still own the data—to which a future descendant will only have full access if they know your username and password and the bill has been paid, or (2) your data is shared and merged into a larger database, in which case it may be altered or merged with incorrect information. You should share your information online, be it on a blog, a website, or with a genealogy website, but make sure you have designated a custodian for that information after you are gone. A good custodian will take care of your family history information and make sure it is migrated into new systems that future generations will enjoy.

Plan For Dissemination

Making sure your family history is circulated among your family members not only protects your information from loss, but also involves your family and ensures that they have their own copies of their history. If you ever have a loss through fire or natural disaster or computer failure or disorganization, you will be able to call upon the members of your family for another copy of your history. So, sharing your family history can serve two purposes. It can preserve your family history for future generations by preserving the physical items that tell your story. It can also preserve your family history by generating family members who are interested in it and vested in making sure that the artifacts and data are kept current and are cared for.

Ask yourself: when my grandchildren and great-grandchildren and great-great-grandchildren want to know about my ancestors, how will they know where to look for the information and artifacts that I have now? I only have one copy of the book my grandfather wrote. A great-great-grandchild of mine may not know that his great uncle Michael inherited my copy of the book. One line of my posterity will have access to my materials and they will be lost to other lines unless I make more copies and distribute them to other family members. I should also make sure that my materials are located in several archives, libraries and online family history sites.

Likewise, my father's cousin who inherited all of my great-grandfather's genealogy books has found himself with a huge responsibility to the rest of our family. Had my dad passed on before I became interested in these books, I would not have known his cousin and may not have even known the books existed. It is a credit to my dad's cousin that he has taken the responsibility of owning these family history treasures seriously. He has carefully photographed each page of all 18 volumes and has worked with family members to create a website where all of the information is accessible to any member of the family. Anyone who is entrusted with family history artifacts should work to make sure all members of the family have access to them.

Ideally photos and documents of your family history should be combined in scrapbook or book format as well as an electronic computer file. Digital copies are inexpensive and some might be tempted to only provide digital copies to future generations, but a hard copy can be more likely to be seen, read, and utilized. Both formats should contain identifying information and a story of your family. Then, as your family grows, digital copies of each item can be sent to family members so that each person has their own copy and can create a hard copy if they wish.

 Library Of Alexandria Rule In Alexandria, Egypt, at the time of Cleopatra, there was an amazing library. The Library of Alexandria may have had hundreds of thousands of books, scrolls, codices, etc. It was a center for learning in the ancient world and scholars came from all over to learn there. Many great scientific and mathematical discoveries that we rely on today were made at the Alexandrian library. According to legend, the Greeks were fighting the people of Alexandria and brought ships in to blockade the harbor. In order to break the blockade, the people of Alexandria set fire to the ships. The fire swept onto land and the Library of Alexandria was burned. All of the knowledge in those books, papyri and codices were lost except for those that had been copied and were stored in other places. In modern times we don't know what was in that library, but we have nowhere near a hundred thousand volumes from that time period. All we have are the precious texts, religious manuscripts and other important materials that had been copied and placed elsewhere.

The story of the Library of Alexandria leaves a strong message for genealogists who want future generations to be able to use their genealogy research work. So much so, that I've created the Library of Alexandria Rule for Genealogists: The more copies there are of your family records, the more likely it is they will survive. If you obey the Library of Alexandria rule, you will share, share, share your family history information.

 Spread Your History Now! Family historians who are actively collecting their family's history are prone to keep telling themselves that they can't share the information they have found yet because it isn't finished. When you know how important your history is to your descendants, you are never going to be finished, so don't wait. Even if you aren't finished, even if they don't seem all that interested yet, even if it goes in the back of a closet and is disregarded, at least it will be there for them later or for someone else who comes across it. Make it easy for your family to come to love their ancestors and readily enjoy the bounty of knowing their roots.

Go Do It

Nurturing a child is the most important job in the world. When parents do their job well, their children are more likely to be secure and grounded largely because of the love they feel in their family. The connection with parents and grandparents is crucial and will reverberate throughout the child's life. Even more far reaching, that connection will resonate into future generations of the family. Family historians know the difference that one person can make in generations to come. One person can be the great turning point in a family. One person can affect many generations, and those family members affected can in turn make a great impact on the world.

A super grandma—or grandpa—can be a huge help to parents. When children grow up in a close knit extended family, they are more likely to be successful adults. Grandma and Grandpa continue to have an impact on the family when they forge close connections with their grandchildren. Whether they live close or far away, whether they care for them daily or see them just once in a while, the extended family society can be an important part of a child's world. Even when there are bumps and bruises in family life, the family is inextricably linked by all their successes and failures, fears, pains, insecurities, joys, and loves. No matter how it plays out, the family is an essential part of our core. Ideally, when a family pulls together, they help each other with the shared goals of fostering the next generation.

Regardless of the structure of your family, you can be like Super Grandma and use family history to connect to your family members and connect them to a healthy future. When you zap the generation gap and link the youth in your family to the Super Grandmas and Super Grandpas in their past (all families have them somewhere in their lines), they can build on the achievements and successes of previous generations. Help your children and grandchildren identify with the super heroes in your family history. Your family's history will bind them tightly to you, and then they can become super heroes themselves.

As you've read this book, you've thought of some specific ideas about how to apply the suggestions here to your own family history. Pick and choose the activities that best fit your family's interests. When you put those ideas into action, the connections you make between the youth in your family and their ancestors will bind all the generations together into one great whole. Make these tight connections a way of life. Use the big family history moments as well as the little ones to create a pattern that will filter down through coming generations. You stand now as the crucial axis in your family. Nourish your family members with their history so that they can become strong and powerful ancestors to future generations. When you do that, you will have changed the world.

What's Next?

Recommended resources to help you connect even more to your family.

Inspire your child Check out Zapthegrandmagap.com for a free .pdf download. Go to Zapthegrandmagap.com/downloads for a free 35 page family history workbook that your children and grandchildren can use to begin recording their own history and what they know about their ancestors along with a pedigree chart to print and fill out.

Boost your momentum Sign up for our 52 weekly emails with more ideas about how to involve your family with their family history. Go to Zapthegrandmagap.com to register. You can unsubscribe anytime though you won't want to. The emails will give you great ideas every week about how to connect with your kids and grandkids.

Power up and take action Check out the other books and resources at Zapthegrandmagap.com/books including the workbook companion to this book and other workbooks to help your children explore their roots. Watch for the continually developing resources for exploring your family history with your children.

Energize with the community Contribute to our blog at zapthegrandmagap.blogspot.com, participate in the Facebook community and share in the Twitter dialogue @zapgrandmagap. Share your great ideas and see what others have been doing to connect to their families in new ways. Zapthegrandmagap.com/connect.

Mark it out Create beautiful displays of your family's history with Family ChartMasters, including the Zap the Grandma Gap chart that you can fill out with your family. Go to Zapthegrandmagap.com/charts.

Tell a friend Help us change the world one family at a time. For information on bulk orders of this book please contact us through Family ChartMasters at 801-87CHART or info@familychartmasters.com.

We would love to hear your comments and success stories. Email janet@zapthegrandmagap.com or write Janet Hovorka, P.O. Box 1080, Pleasant Grove, Utah 84062.

About the Author

Janet Hovorka serves as the development director of two major entities—the Family ChartMasters company and the Hovorka family. Almost 10 years ago, with her husband Kim (CEO), Janet helped found Family ChartMasters, a genealogy chart printing service (www.familychartmasters.com). The company prides itself on being able to print any kind of genealogy chart, from beautiful fine art pieces to 600-foot family reunion draft charts. Family ChartMasters has printed some amazing charts over the years. They are official printers for most of the genealogy software and database companies. Family ChartMasters has won Family Tree Magazine's Editor's Choice and 101 Best Website awards as well as FamilySearch software awards in both years they've been awarded.

Family ChartMasters came about when Janet inherited a large amount of genealogy from her sister, mother and grandmother, all avid genealogists. As she explored and cataloged it, she tried several times to get "the bigger picture" by creating her own charts to figure out how her family was all related. Luckily she was married to a sweet, generous man who knew how to print large maps so he set about trying to help her. When Kim and Janet first began to print charts for other people, they only wanted to print working charts--to write on and add more information --to help genealogists with their research. Janet didn't want to let anyone frame a chart and say their genealogy was "all done" -- a personal pet peeve. But eventually, since they branched into decorative charts, Janet has become very passionate about keeping family history out where you can see it every day, where it will can inspire you and enrich your life. The Family

ChartMasters motto is "Share, Inspire, Honor." They help family history researchers share their family history with others, inspire themselves and their families with the great stories and images of the people who came before them, and honor their ancestors by keeping their memories alive.

As part of Family ChartMasters, Janet writes the company blog and has become known as the Chart Chick (www.thechartchick.com). Janet has had a wonderful time becoming immersed in the genealogy community and especially the social networking genealogy crowd. She loves the people she gets to work with. They are good, passionate, hard working people who care about family history as much as she does. Janet is currently serving as President of the Utah Genealogical Association and in traveling to genealogy conferences she has presented hundreds of lectures across the U.S. and in Great Britain. Janet loves traveling to genealogy conferences and working with genealogists--they are truly a family.

As Family ChartMasters has developed and Janet has worked with genealogists all over the world, she has become very passionate about the value of having your family history displayed in your home. As you'll find in the pages of this book, she honestly believes family history could save the world. Family ChartMasters is working to give genealogists the tools to involve their family in their family history research. The visual representation of a family, especially a beautiful chart with pictures and stories, is a powerful communication tool about how a family has developed through the years and moved through the world. Janet feels like she is a genealogy evangelist. She loves to draw casual observers into their family's history and create curiosity about the powerful forces that have come to shape their lives. Janet is very pleased to be able to help families across the world connect to each other and to their past. Family Chartmasters has created thousands of beautiful representations of family history, reminders of the generations that make a family and of the connections we all have to our past.

But more important than all of that...Janet is the mother of her family. She is the development director, creator and organizer of the world in which 5 people spin. Her husband and three children are the center of her life. They are the only beings that make her truly happy, and the beings that can cause her the greatest pain. The state of the home they live in, and the organization of their lives, largely rests on her as the mother of the family. She is in charge of nutrition; she organizes the cleaning; she is in charge of shopping and never-ending errands. She oversees the yardwork, the scheduling, the parties, the schoolwork, the activities and myriad other aspects in the family's world. Along with her husband Kim, she has completed 16 years of intense experience in child care that grows more complicated and gives her more satisfaction with every passing year. By some calculations her efforts at home are worth over $500,000 a year, though the work is much harder and much more rewarding than that measly compensation would suggest.

At Family ChartMasters Janet has employees who can run the company even better than she can but no one else can be the mother of her family. For better or for worse, she is theirs and they are hers. Some days the children, and even occasionally her husband, would rather turn her in for a newer, cuter, nicer model, but they really can't. She will always be their mother, and she will always be the mother of her husband's children. The most important work Janet can ever do in this life is to raise her three children to successful adulthood. She is doing her best every day to fulfill that incredible responsibility.

5723

Made in the USA
Lexington, KY
01 February 2019